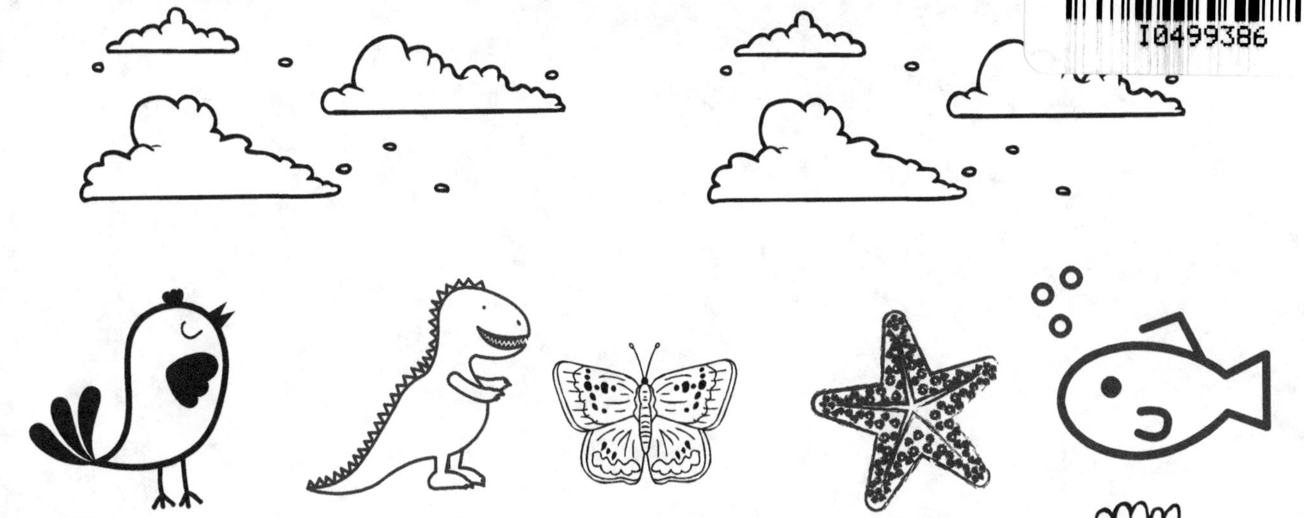

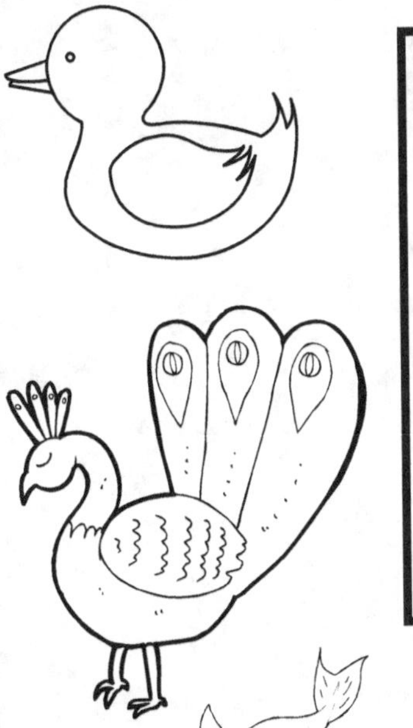

This Book Belongs To

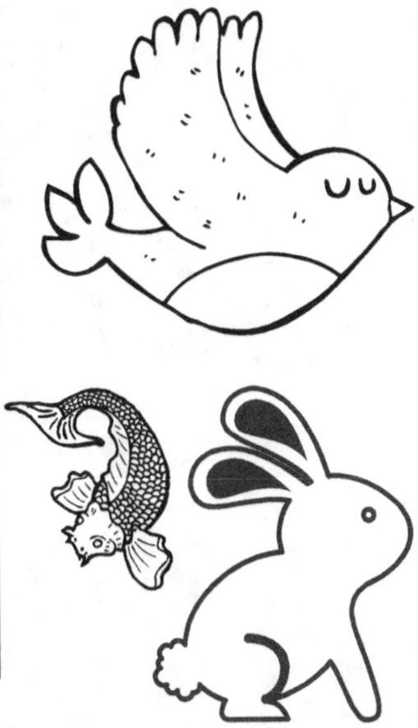

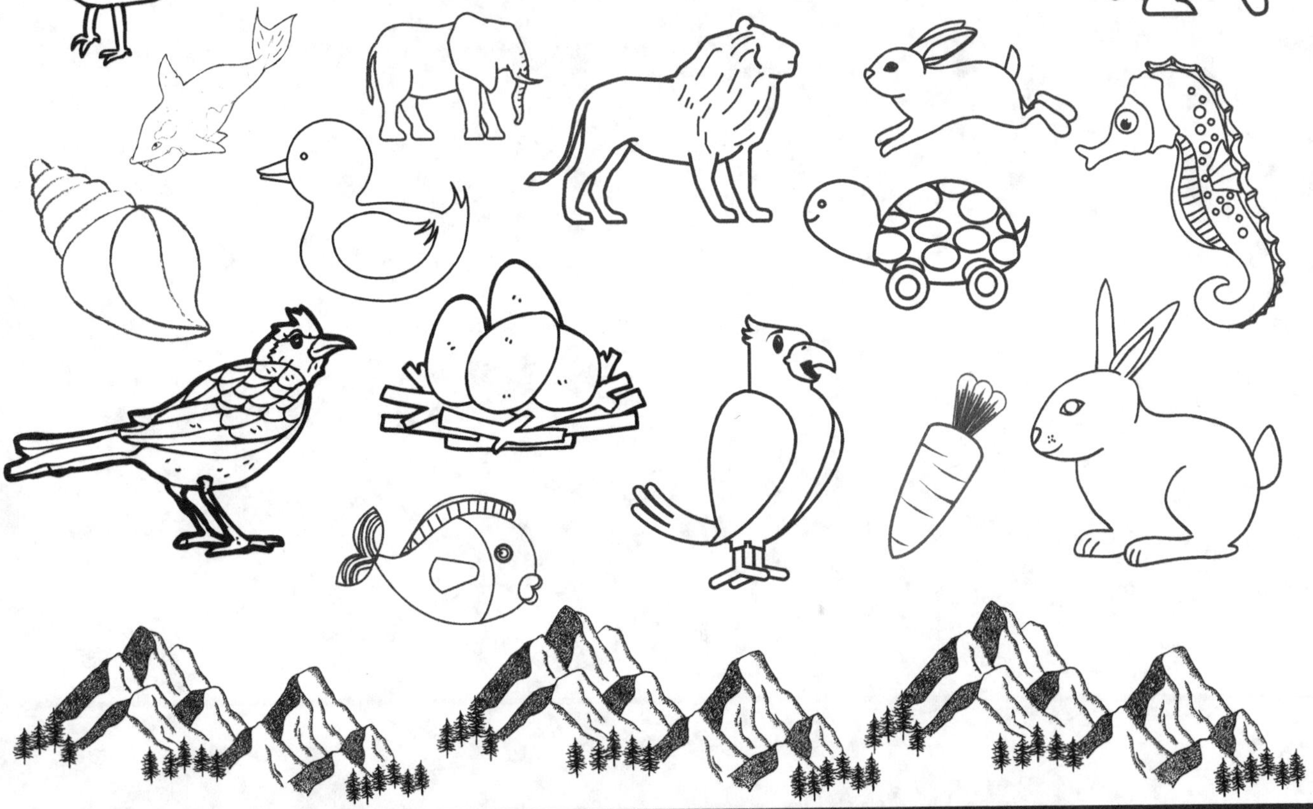

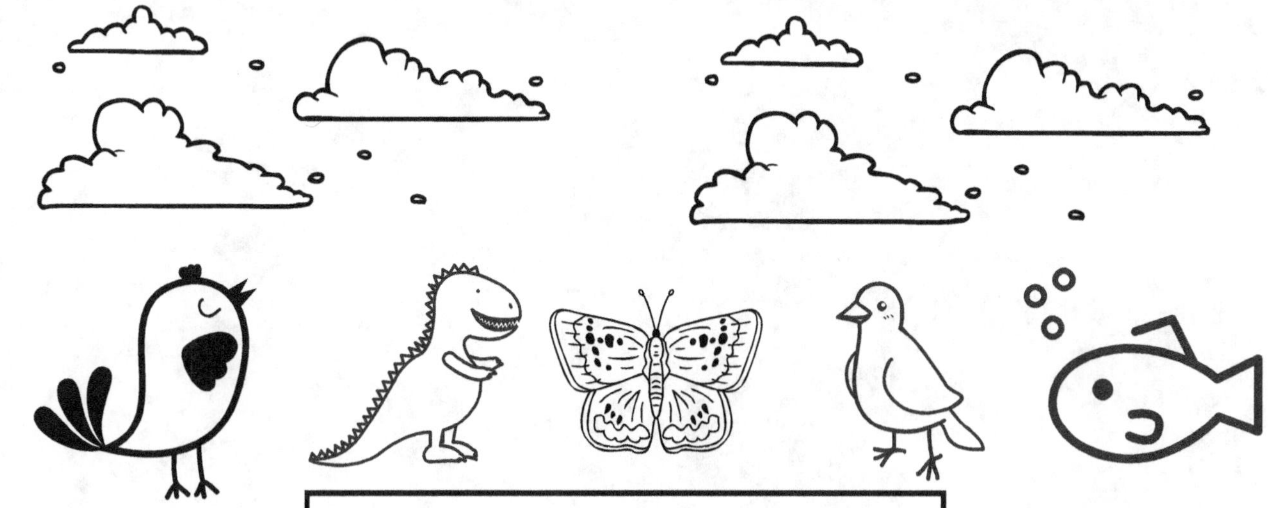

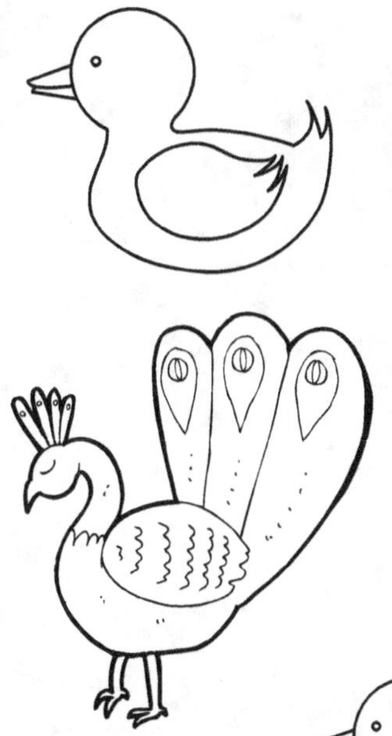

Animal Coloring Book

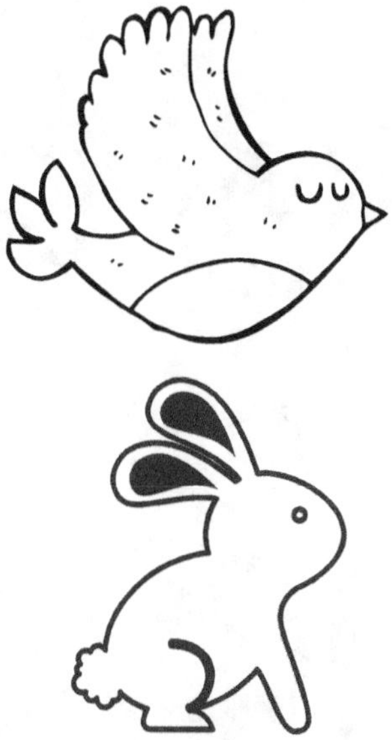

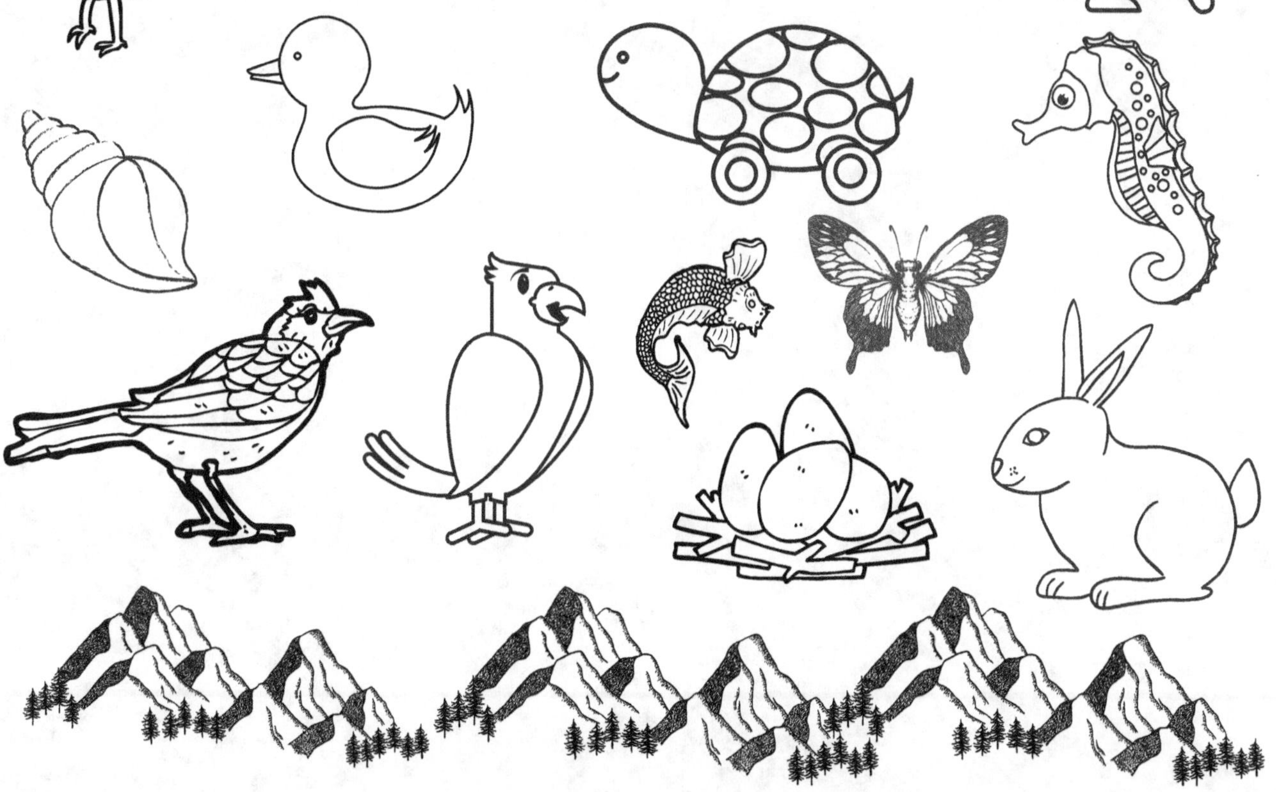

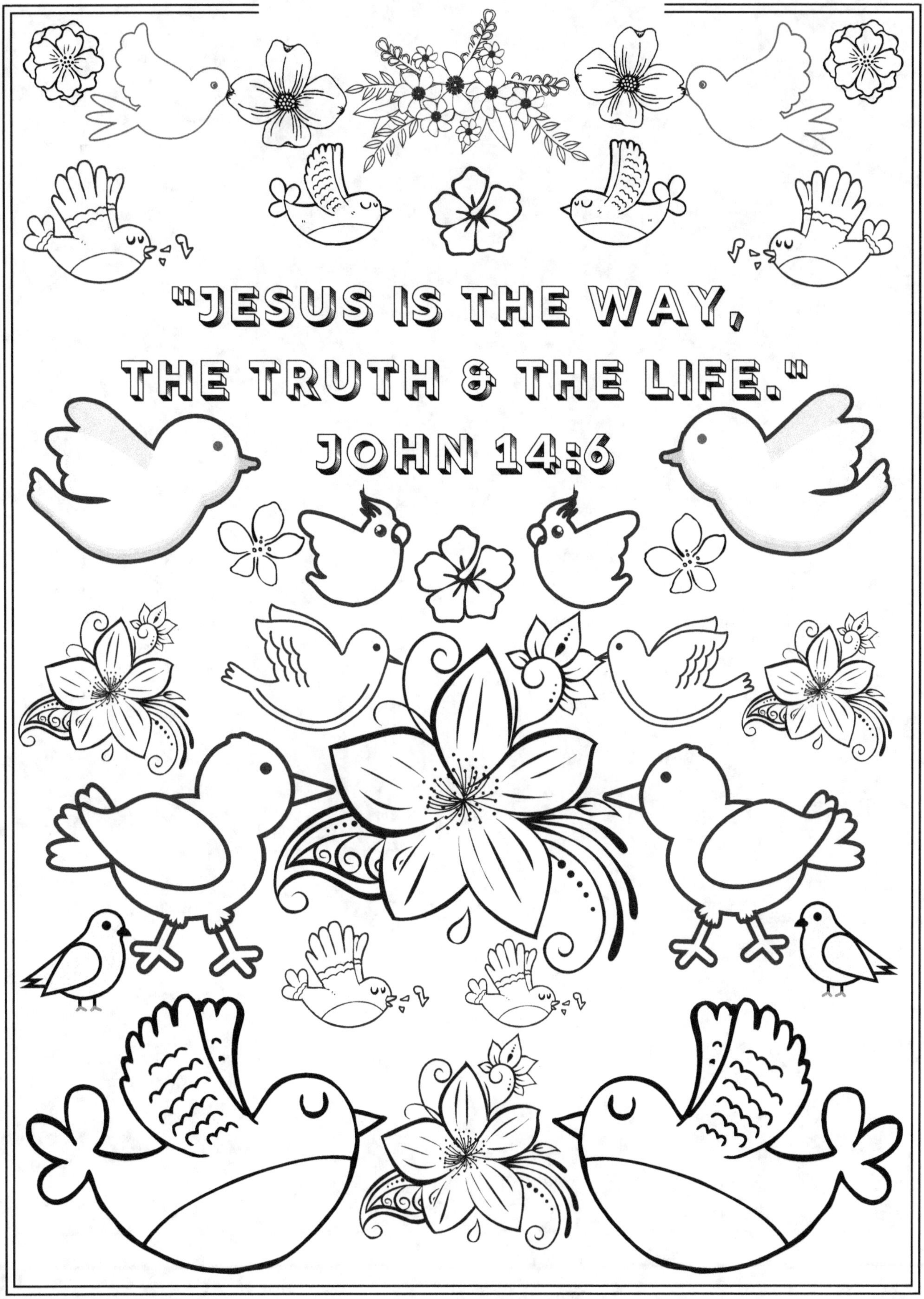
"JESUS IS THE WAY,
THE TRUTH & THE LIFE."
JOHN 14:6

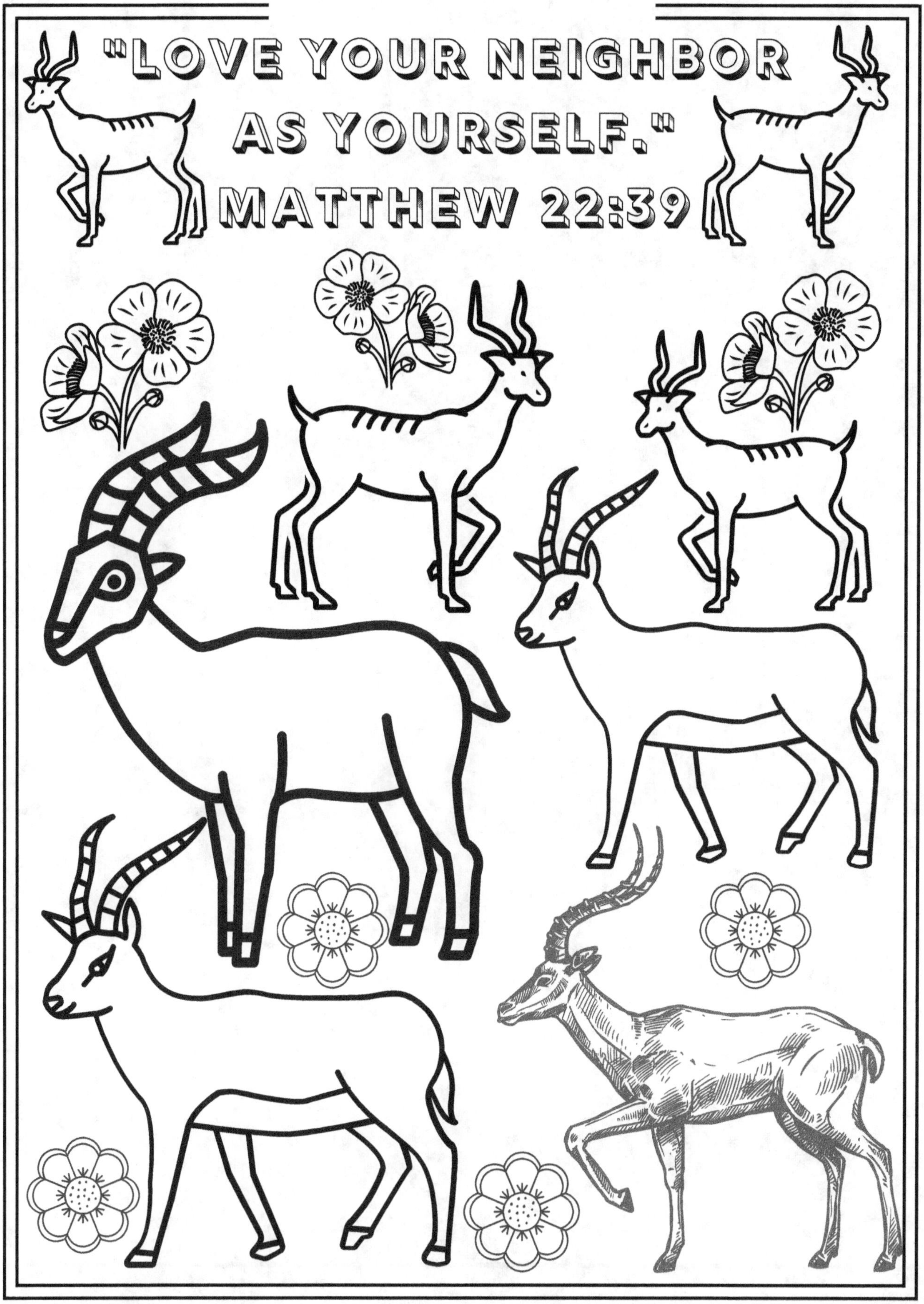
"LOVE YOUR NEIGHBOR
AS YOURSELF."
MATTHEW 22:39

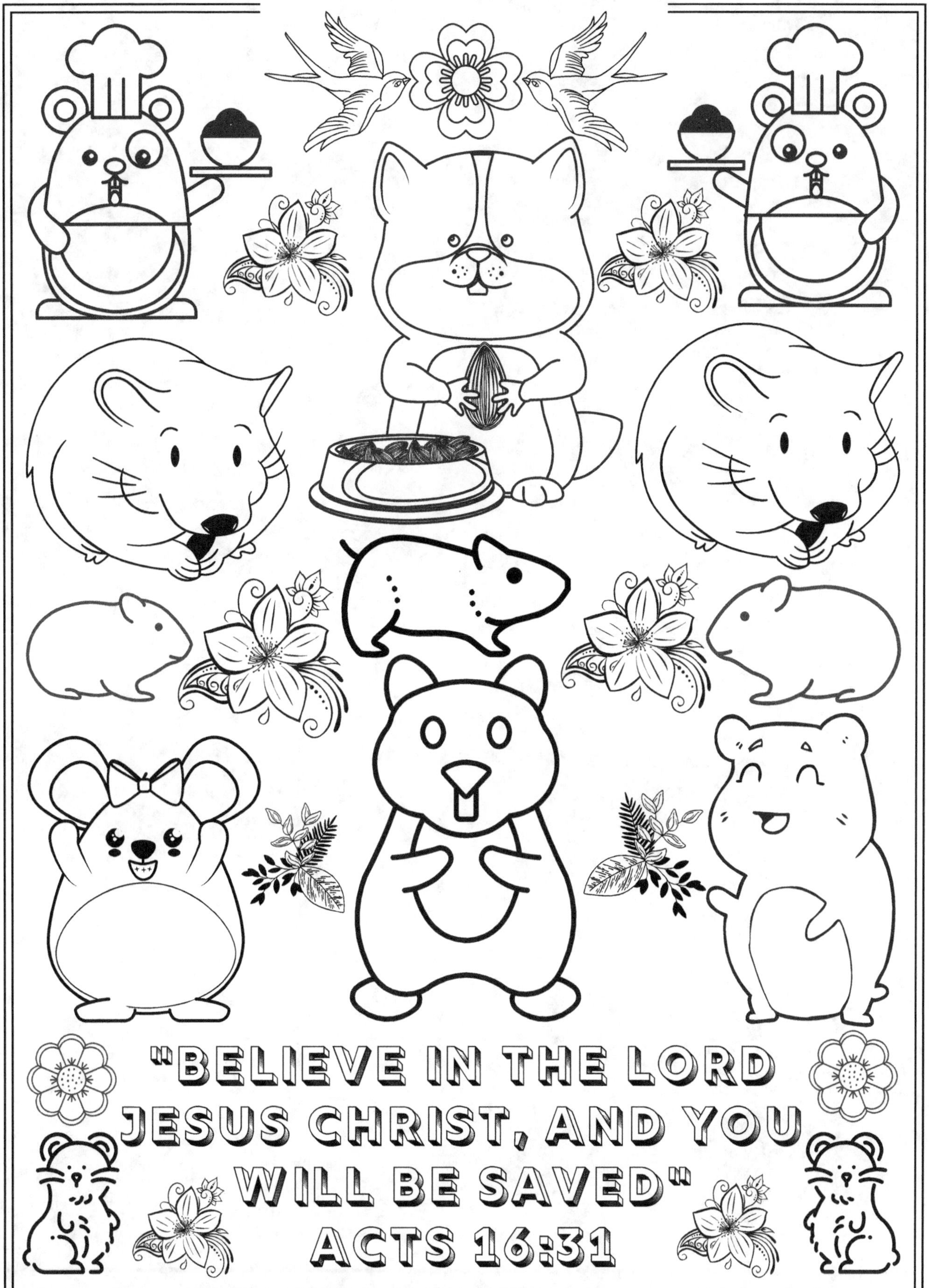
"BELIEVE IN THE LORD
JESUS CHRIST, AND YOU
WILL BE SAVED"
ACTS 16:31

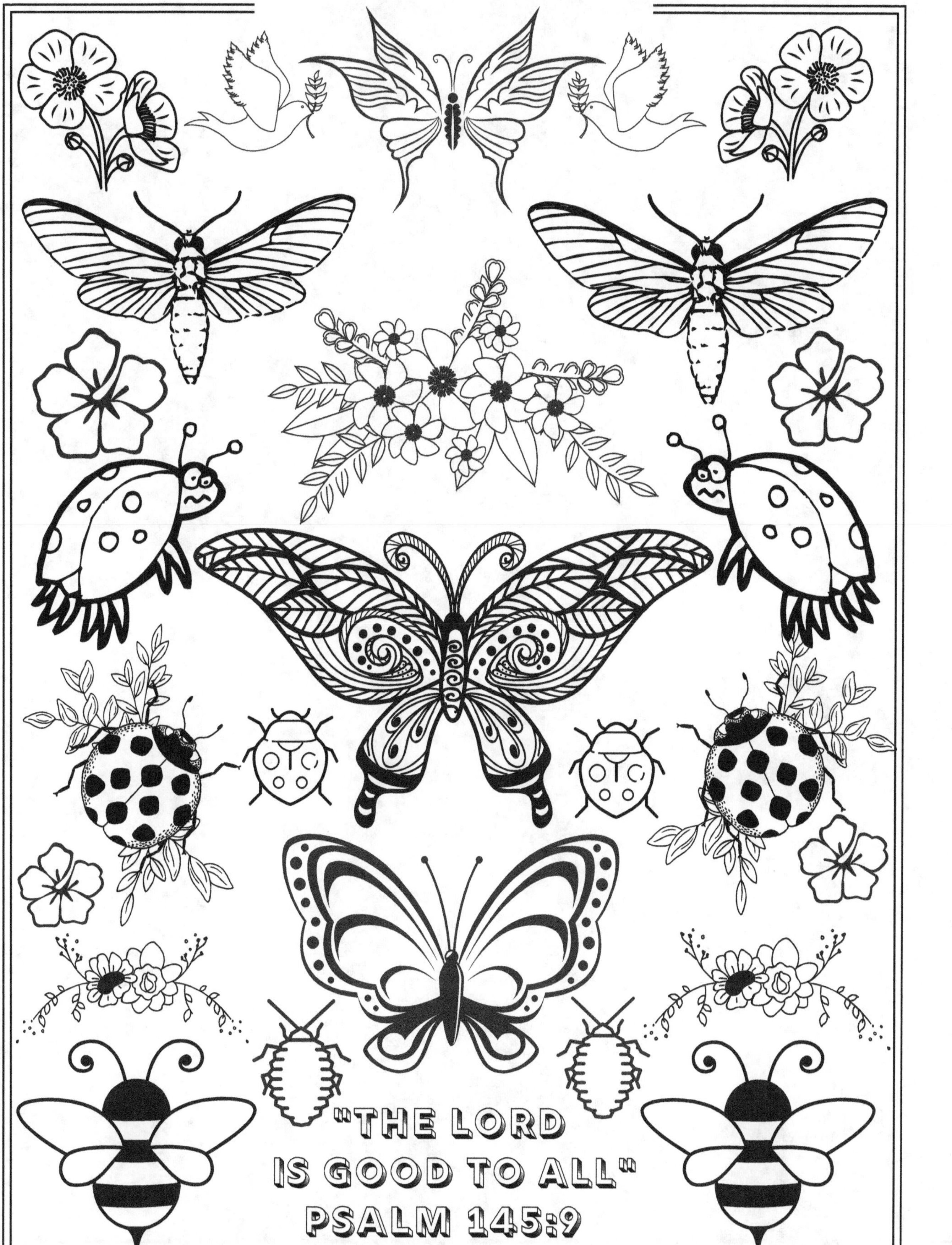
"THE LORD
IS GOOD TO ALL"
PSALM 145:9

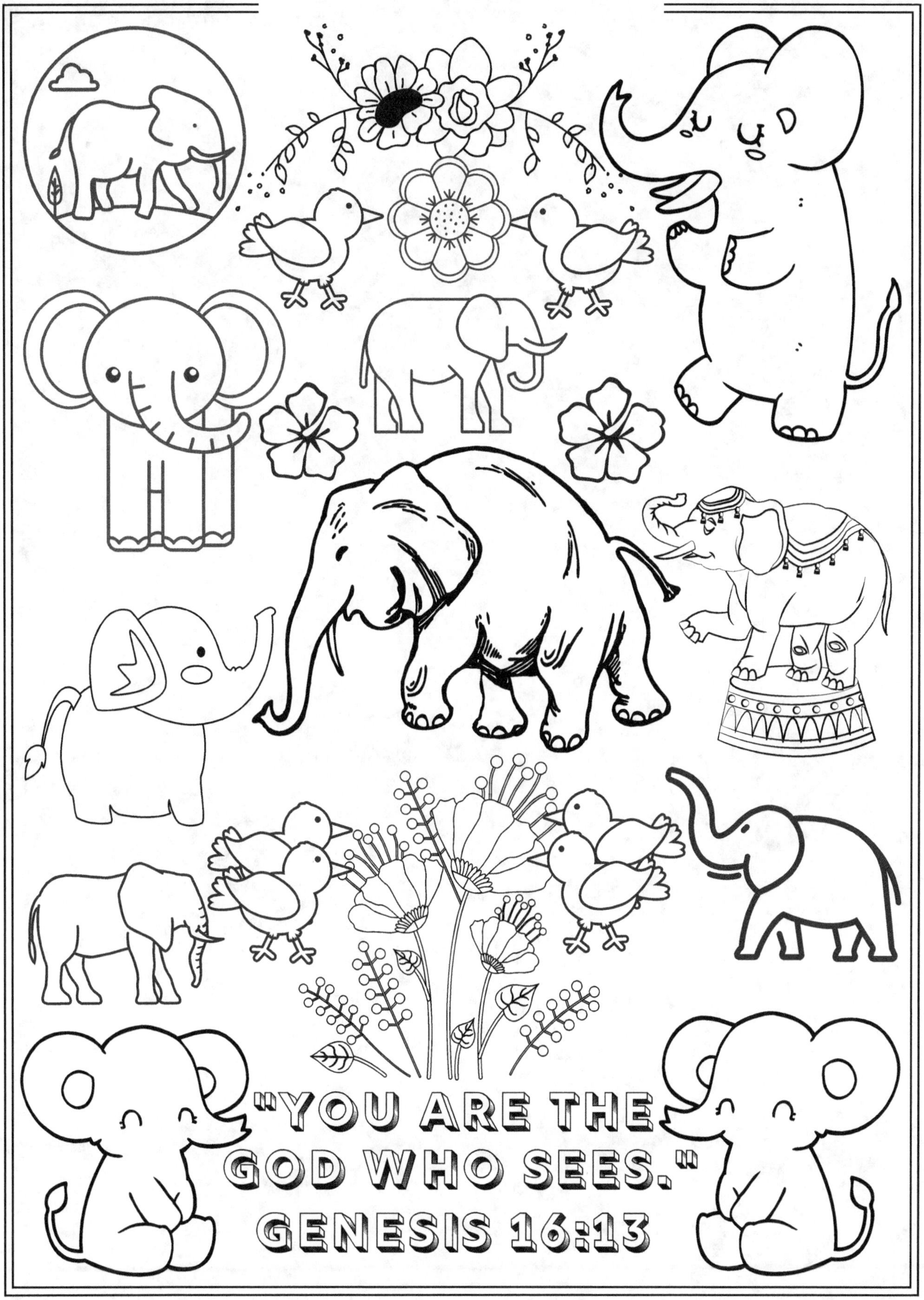
"YOU ARE THE
GOD WHO SEES."
GENESIS 16:13

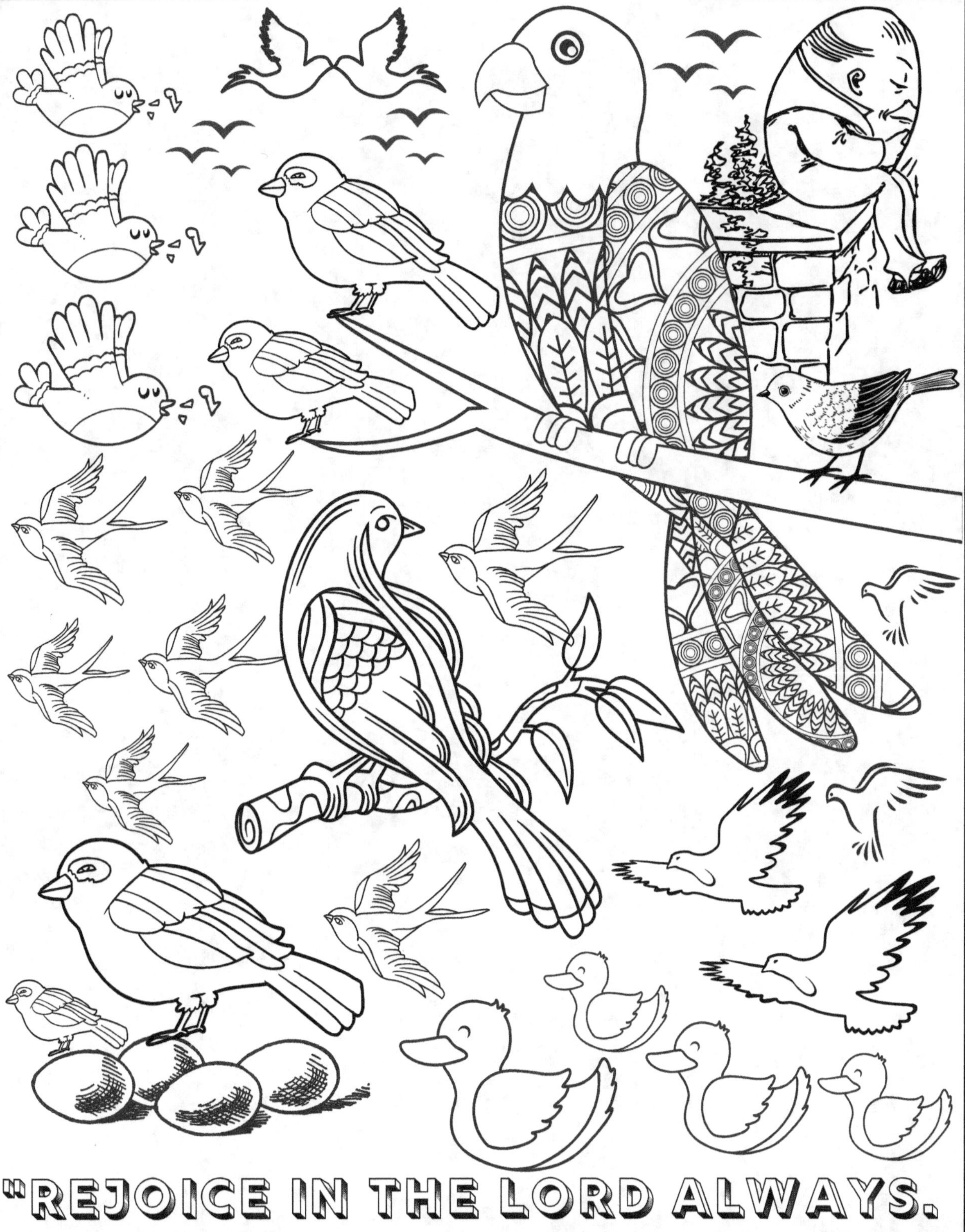

"REJOICE IN THE LORD ALWAYS.
I WILL SAY IT AGAIN: REJOICE!"
PHILIPPIANS 4:4

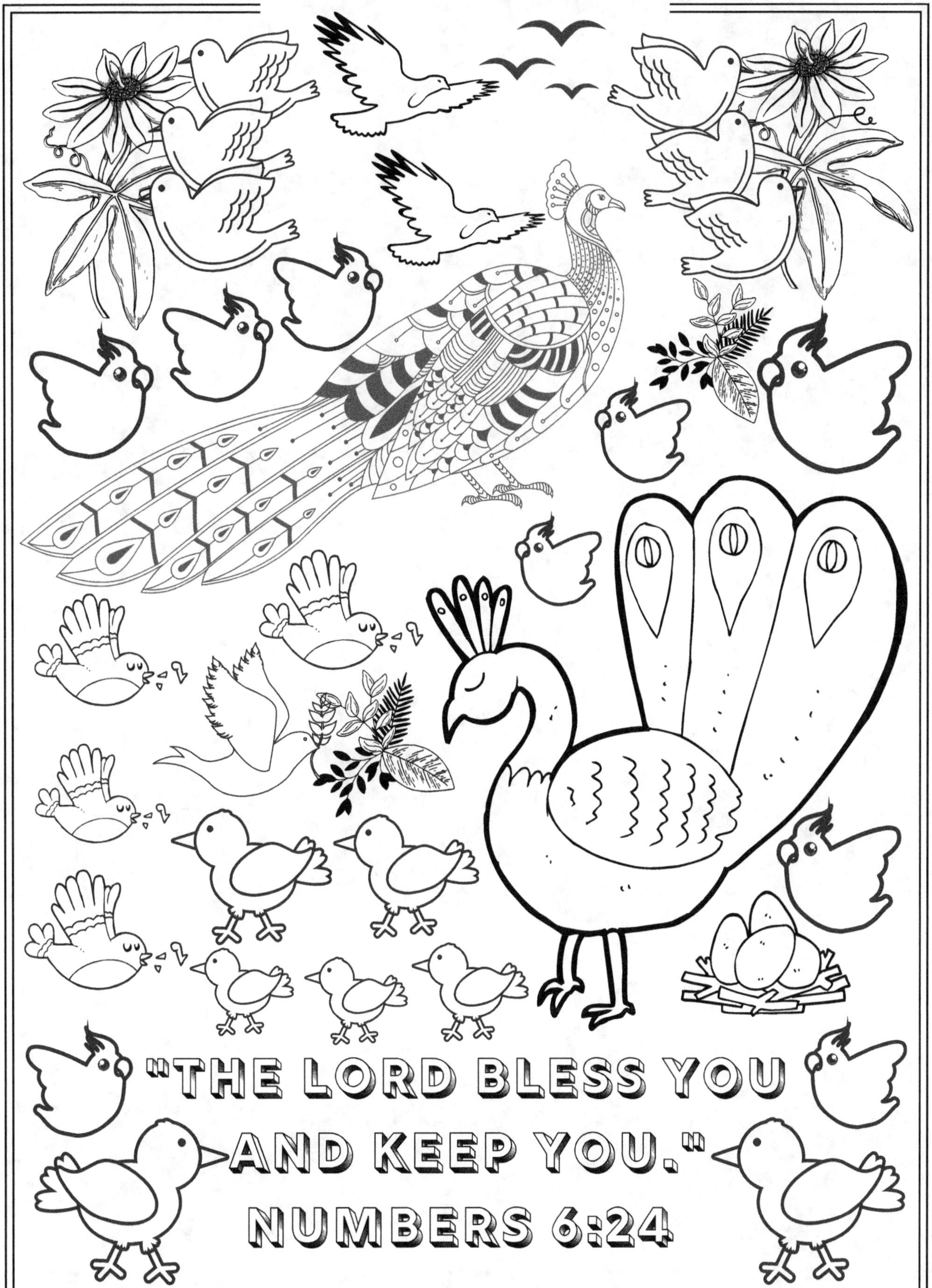
"THE LORD BLESS YOU
AND KEEP YOU."
NUMBERS 6:24

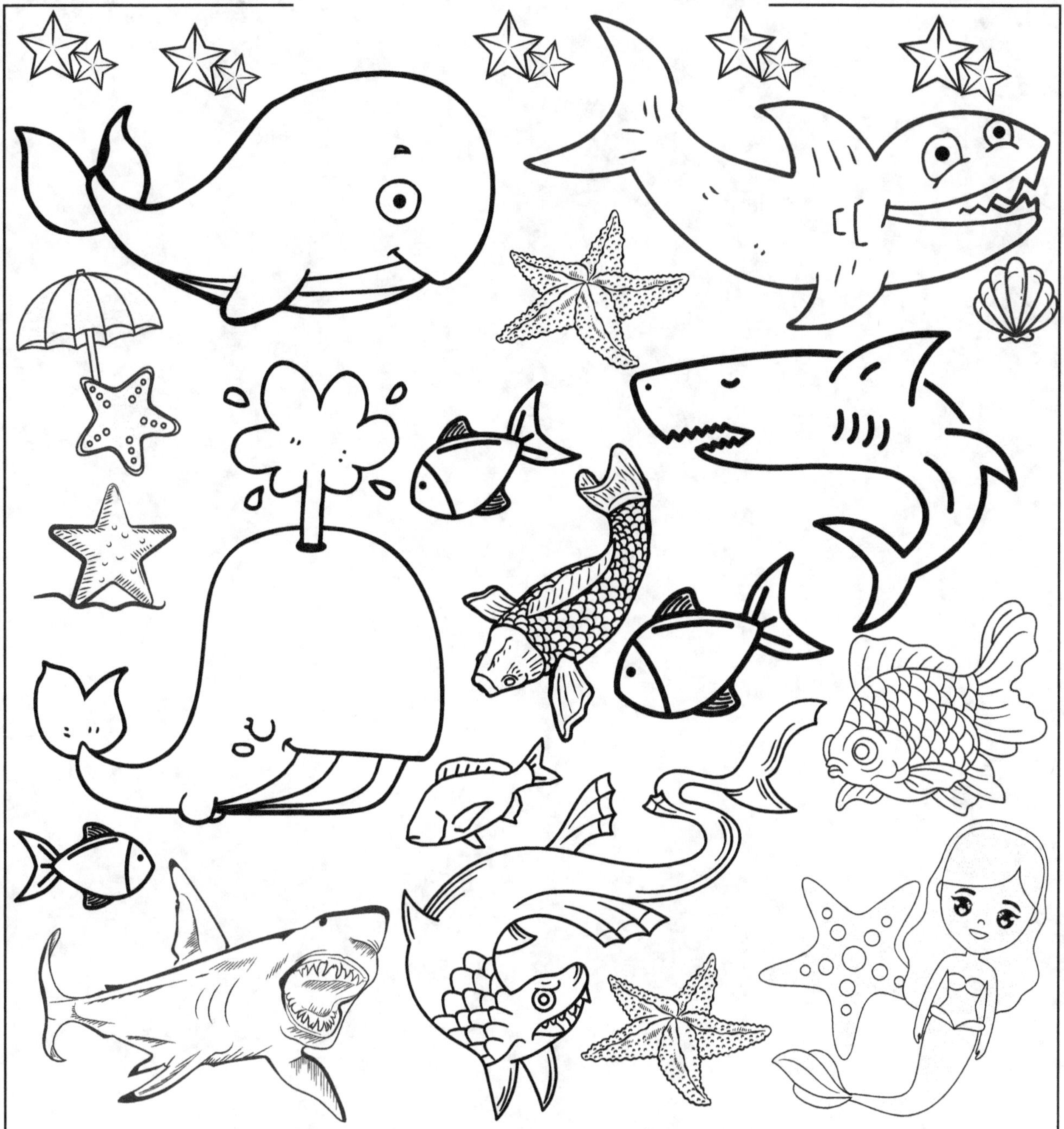

"SET YOUR MINDS
ON THINGS ABOVE,
NOT ON EARTHLY THINGS."
COLOSSIANS 3:2

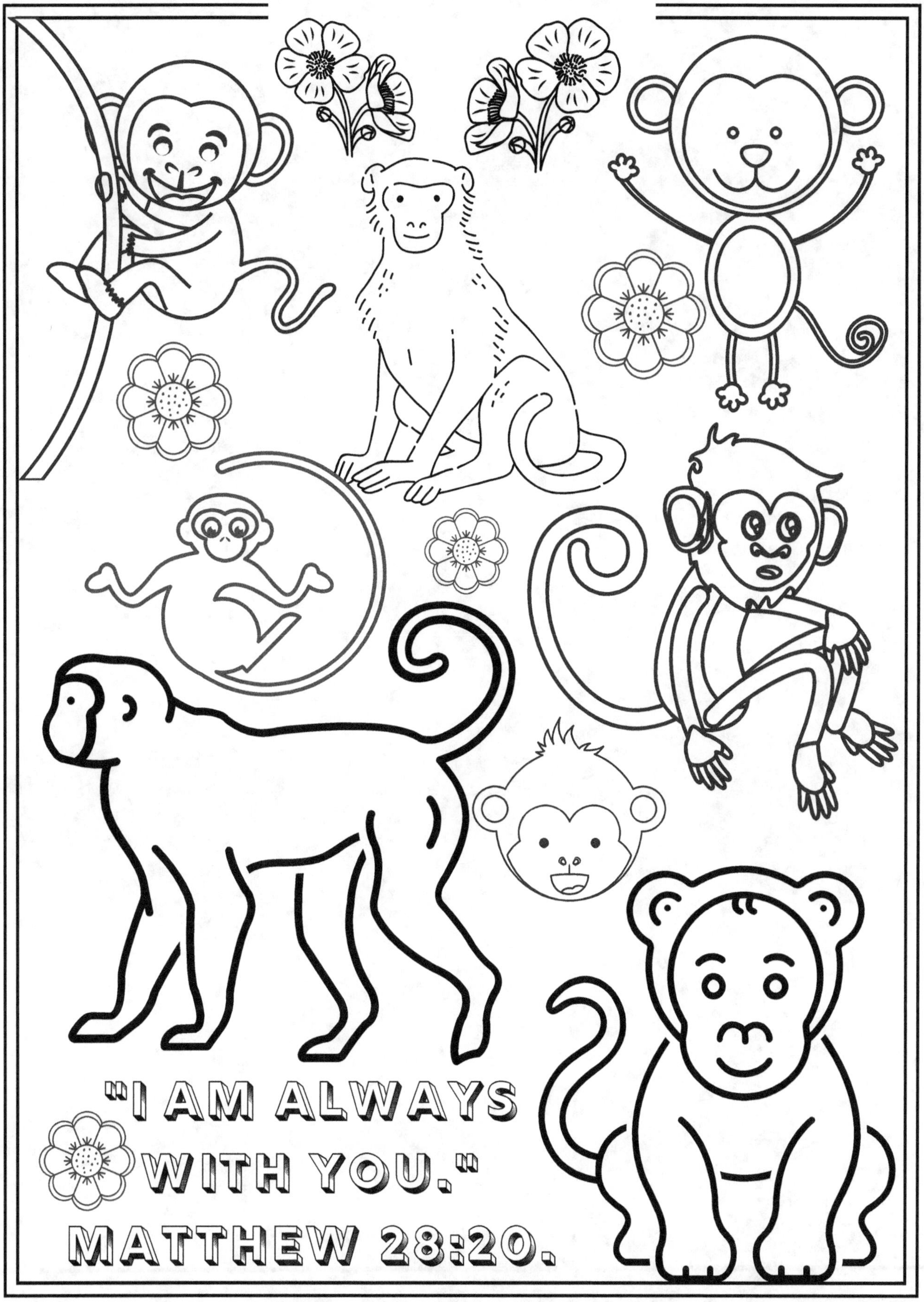
"I AM ALWAYS
WITH YOU."
MATTHEW 28:20.

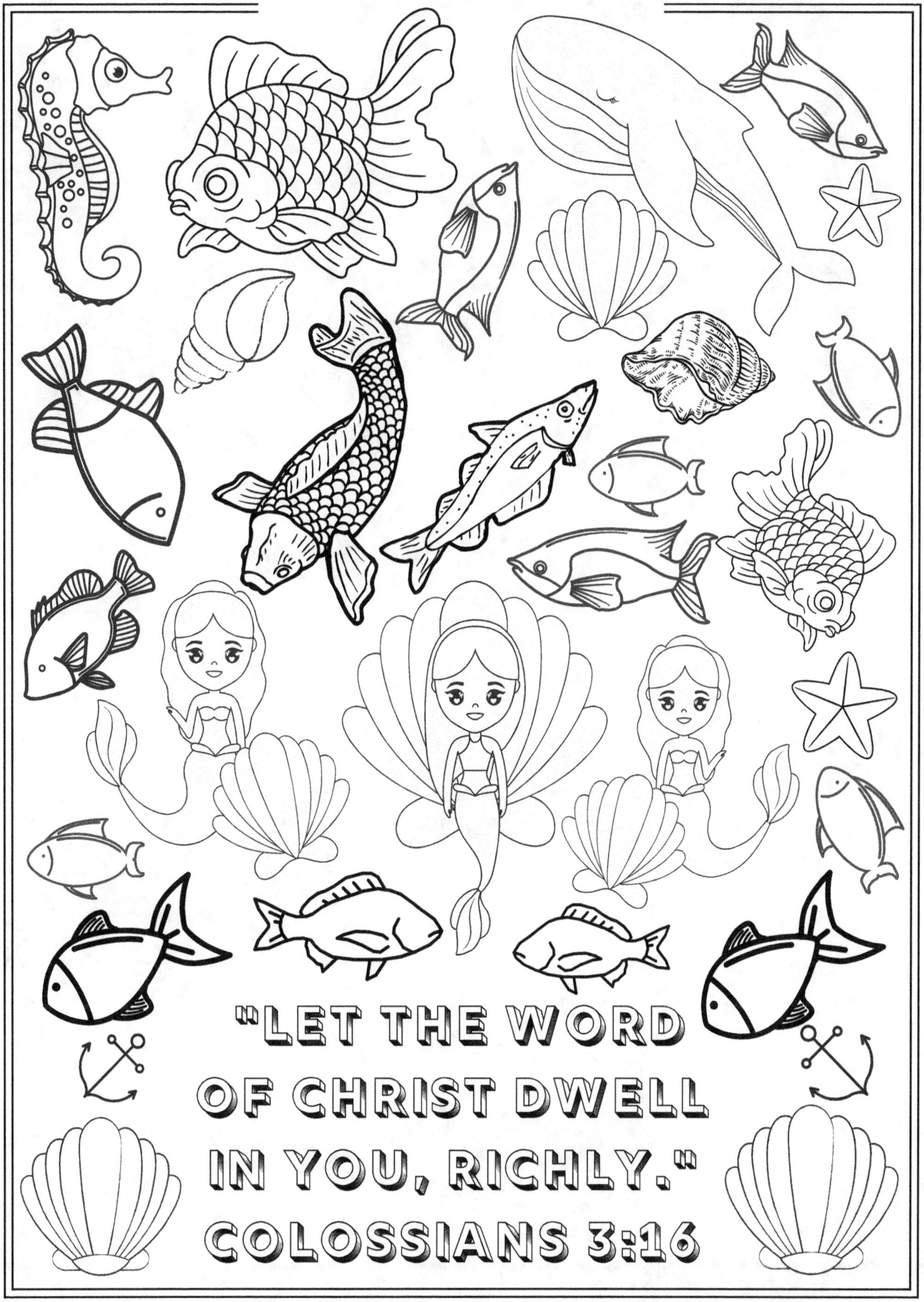
"LET THE WORD
OF CHRIST DWELL
IN YOU, RICHLY."
COLOSSIANS 3:16

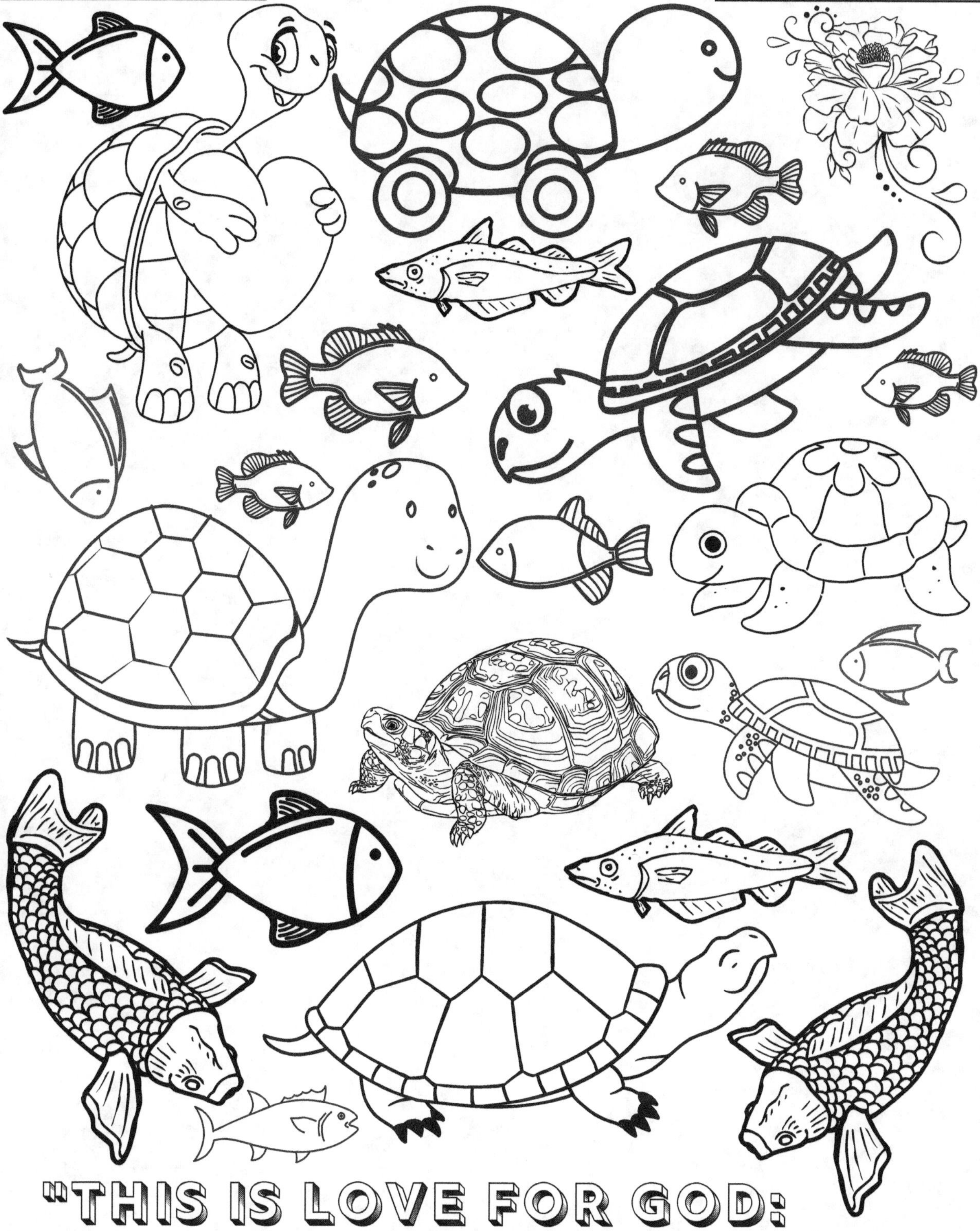

"THIS IS LOVE FOR GOD:
TO OBEY HIS COMMANDS."
1 JOHN 5:3

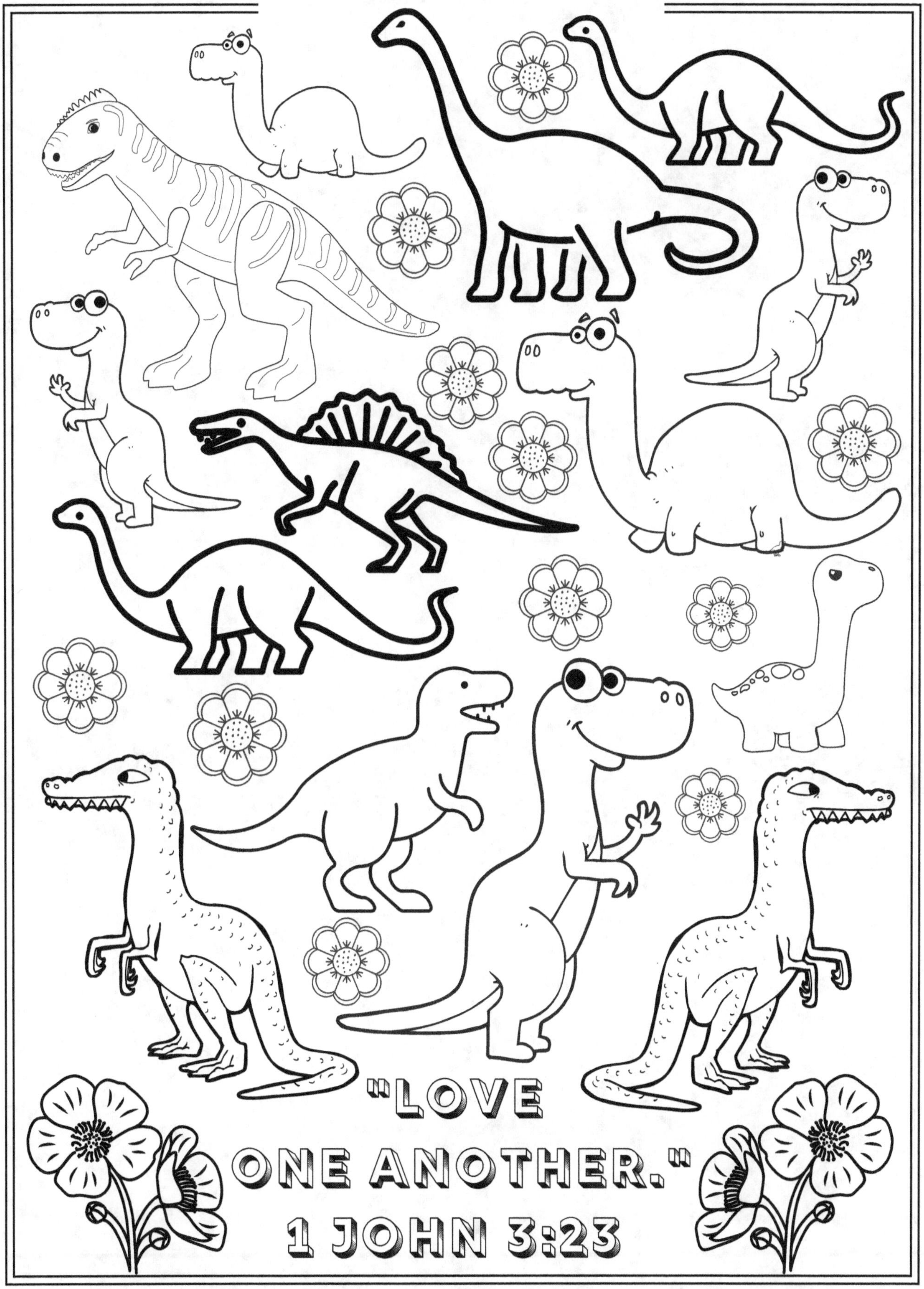
"LOVE
ONE ANOTHER."
1 JOHN 3:23

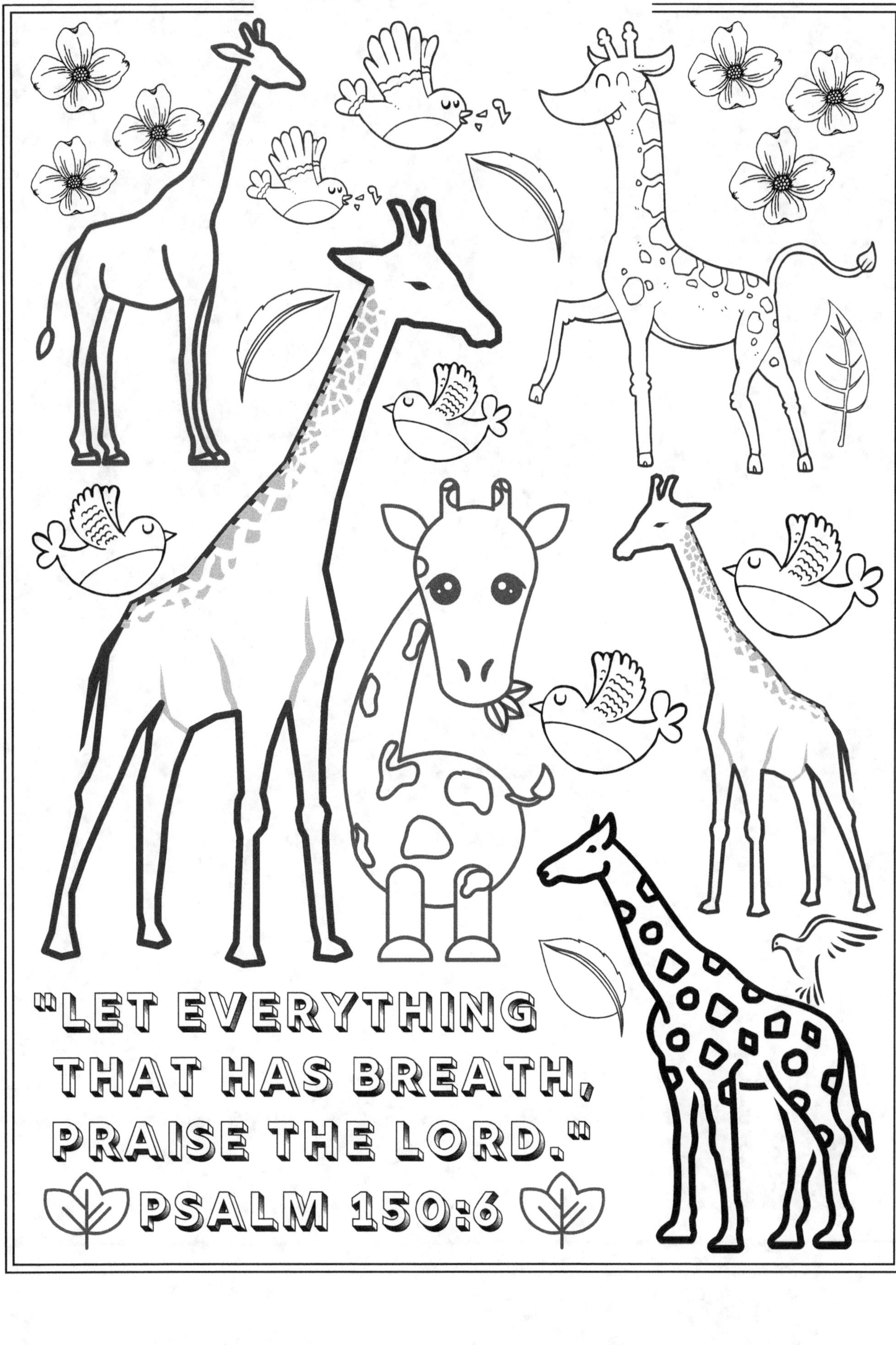
"LET EVERYTHING THAT HAS BREATH, PRAISE THE LORD."
PSALM 150:6

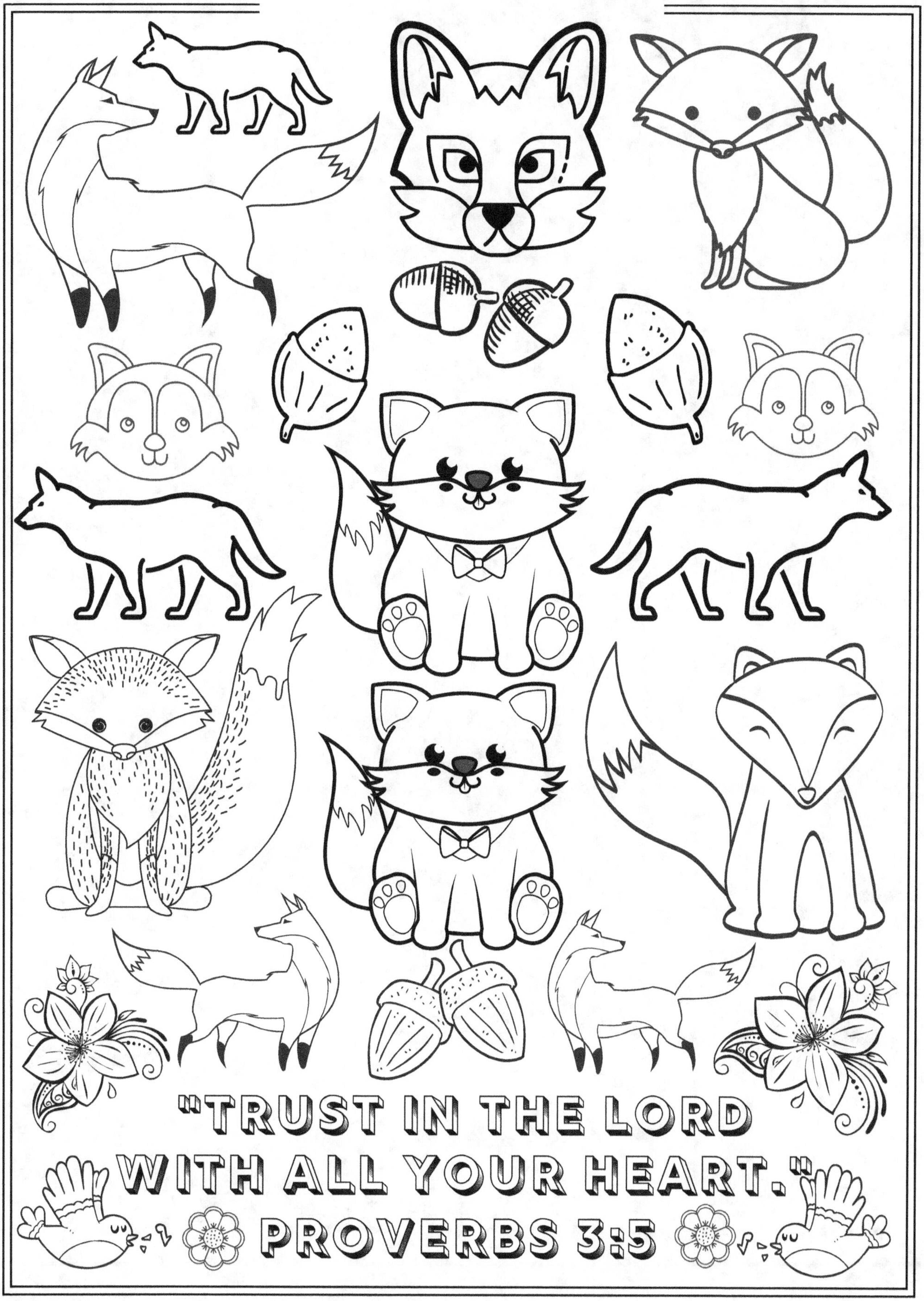
"TRUST IN THE LORD
WITH ALL YOUR HEART."
PROVERBS 3:5

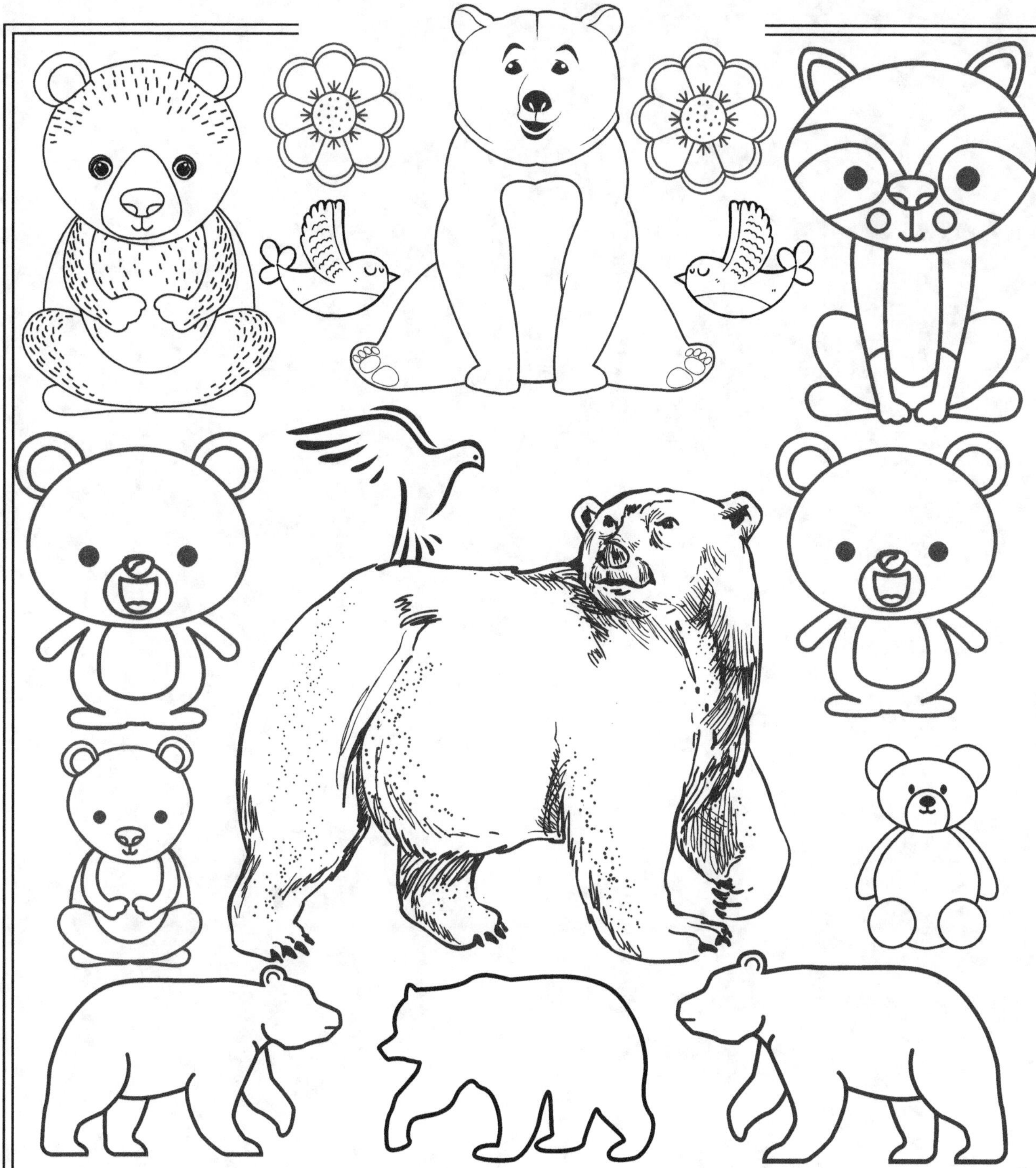

"EVERYONE WHO CALLS ON THE NAME OF THE LORD WILL BE SAVED."

ROMANS 10:13

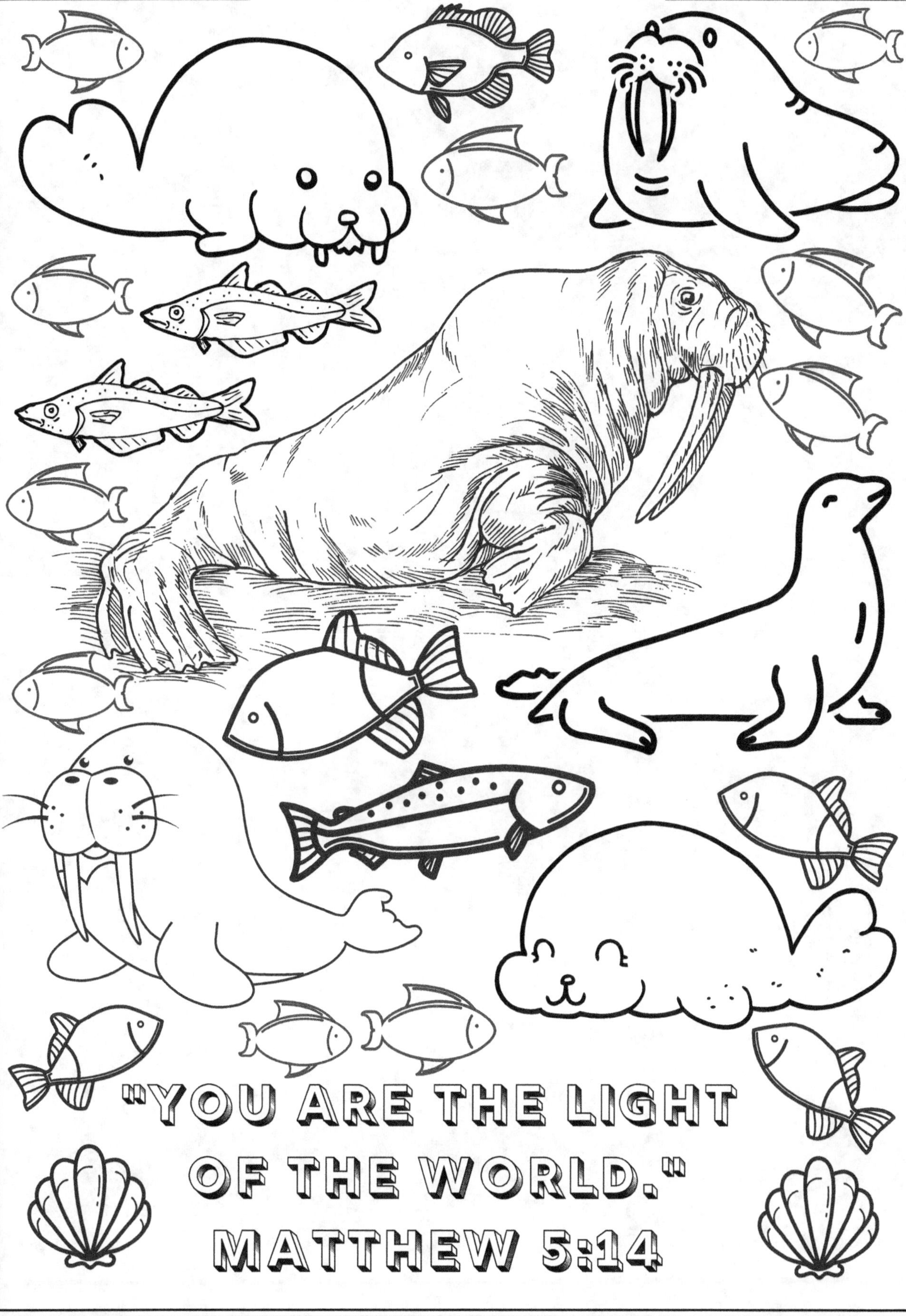

"YOU ARE THE LIGHT
OF THE WORLD."
MATTHEW 5:14

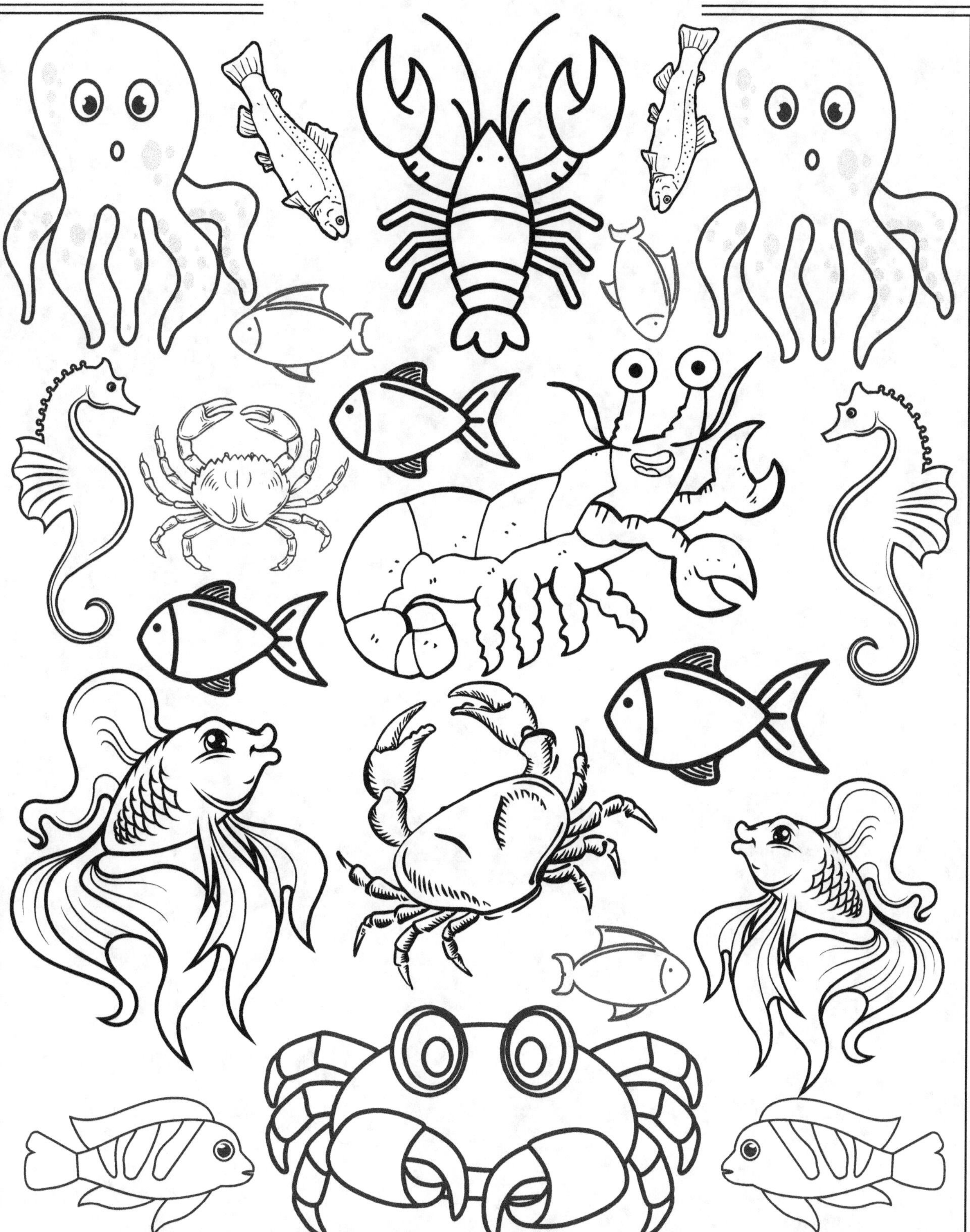

"THE LORD IS GOOD TO ALL."

PSALM 145:9

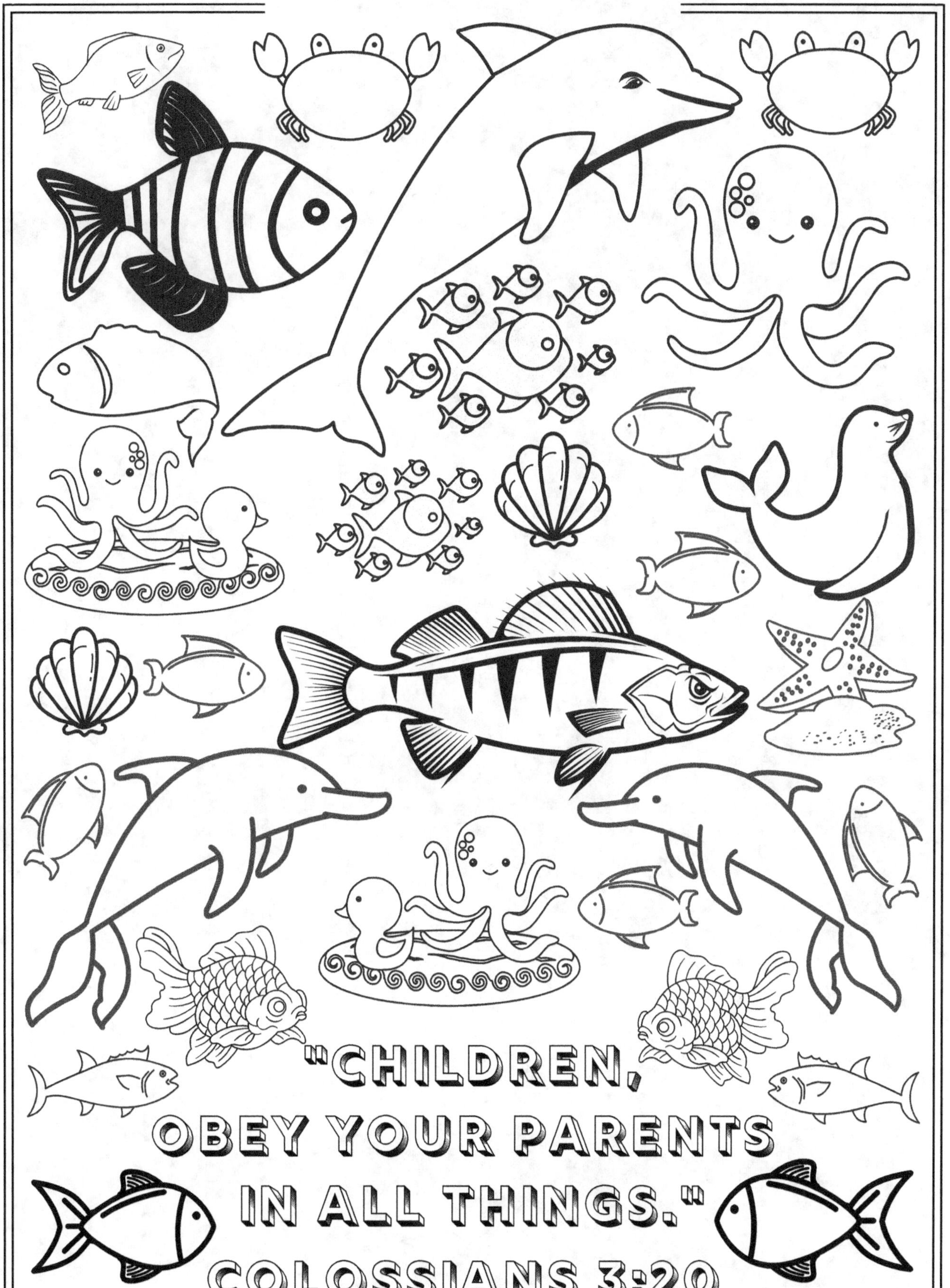
"CHILDREN,
OBEY YOUR PARENTS
IN ALL THINGS."
COLOSSIANS 3:20

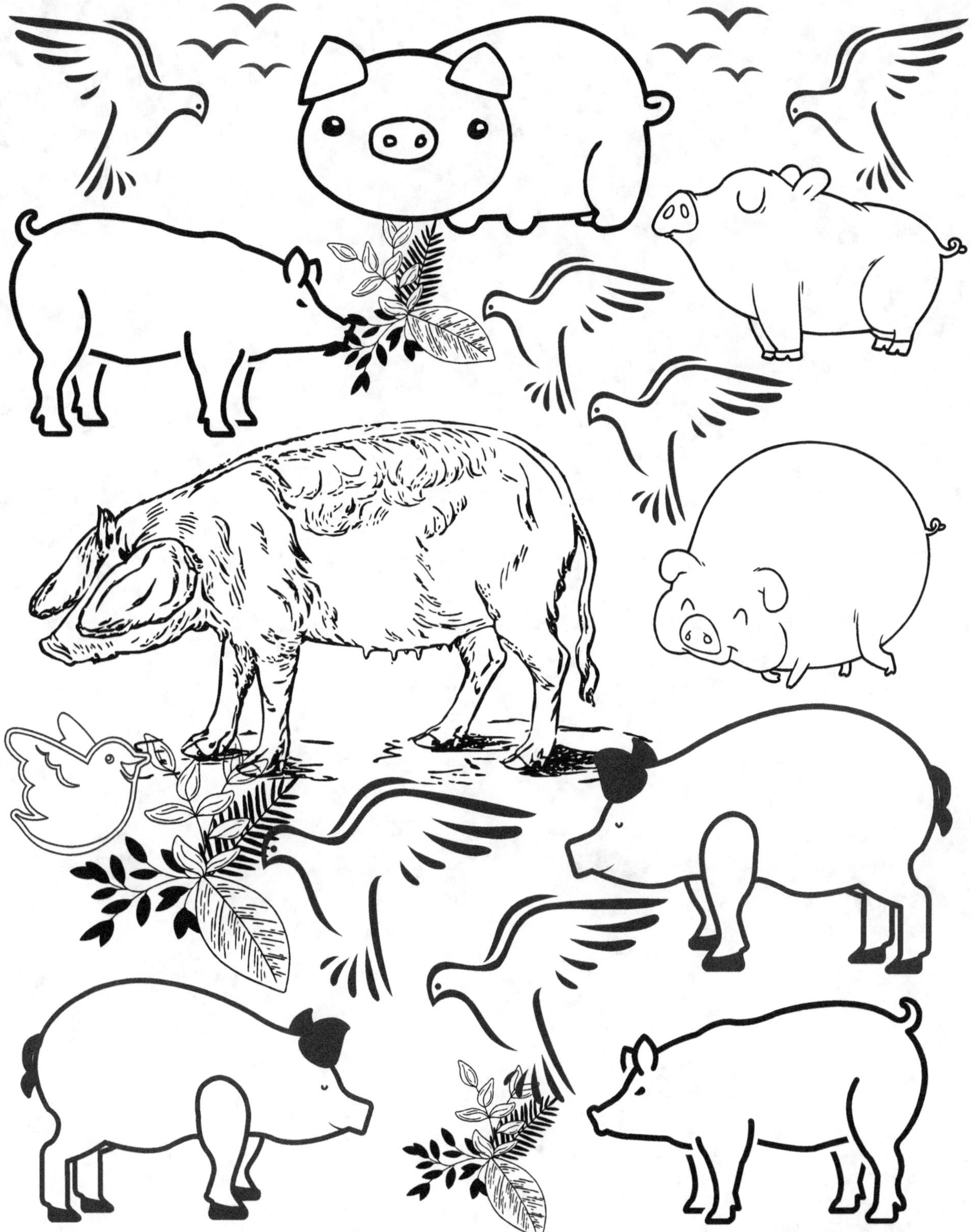

"I AM WITH YOU ALWAYS."

MATTHEW 28:20

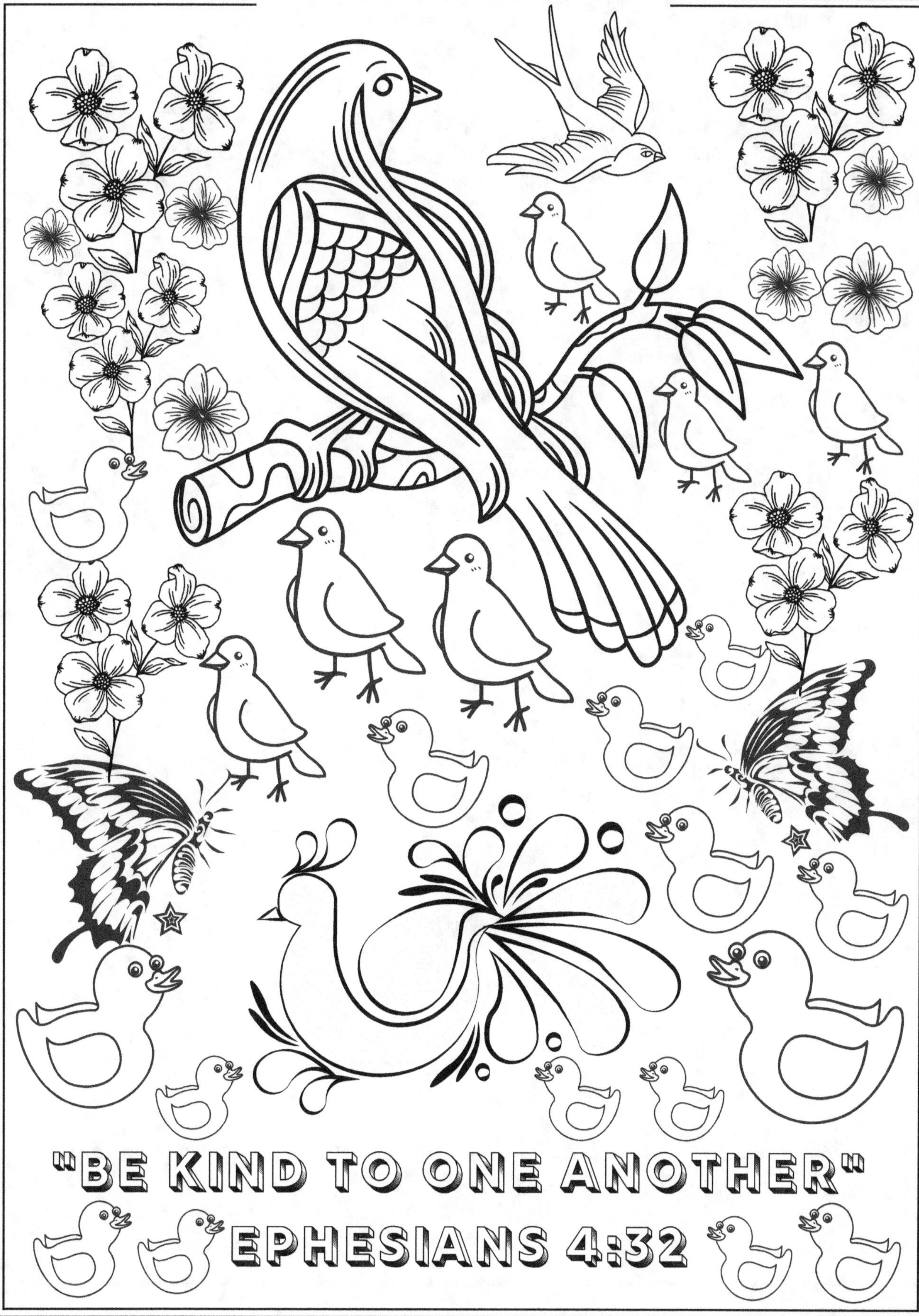

"BE KIND TO ONE ANOTHER"

EPHESIANS 4:32

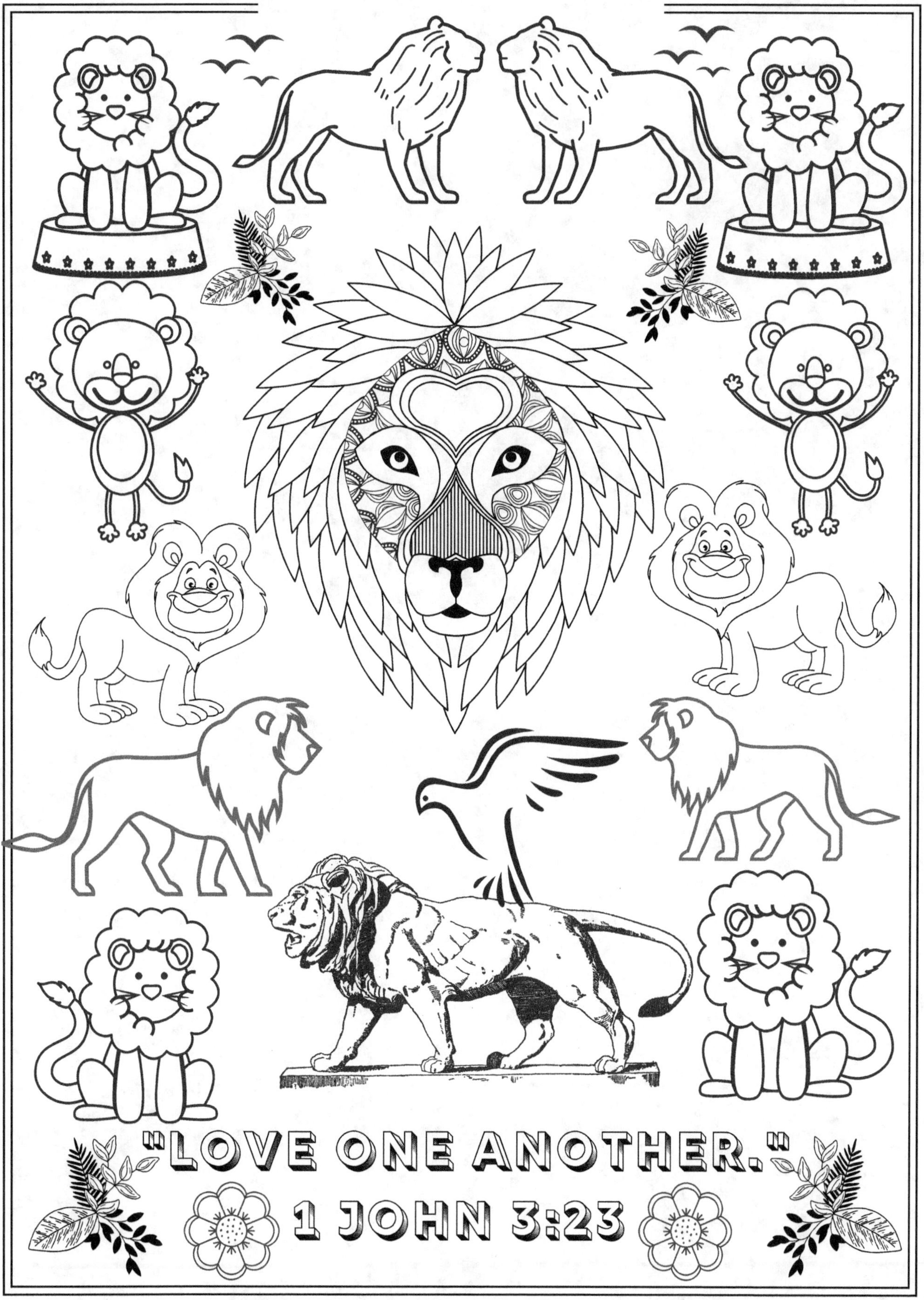

"LOVE ONE ANOTHER."

1 JOHN 3:23

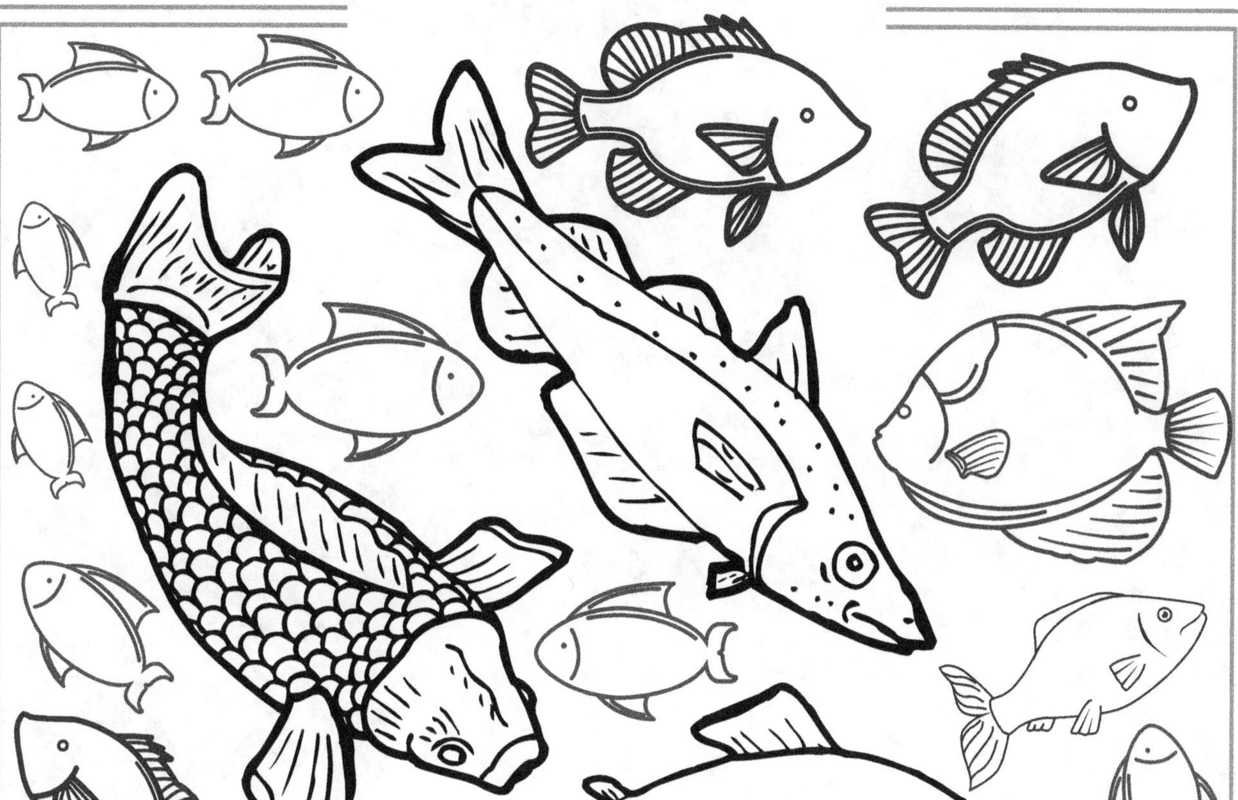

"WHENEVER I AM AFRAID,
I WILL TRUST IN YOU, LORD."

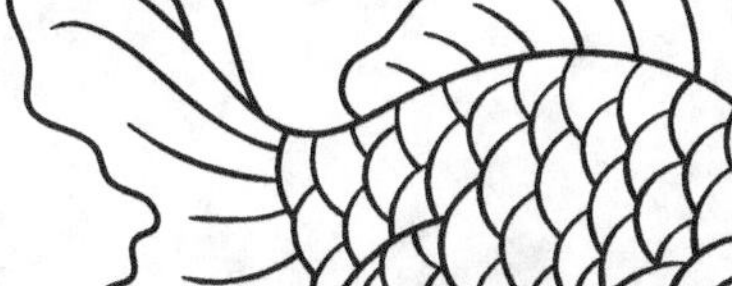

PSALM 56:3

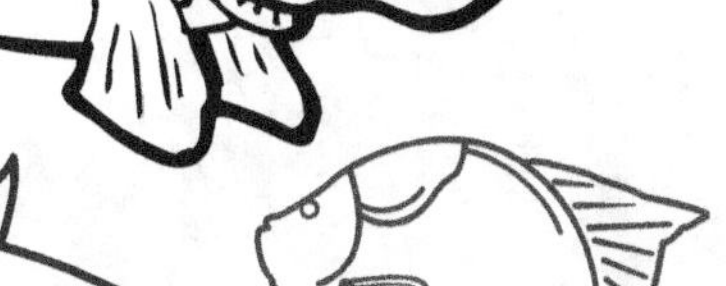

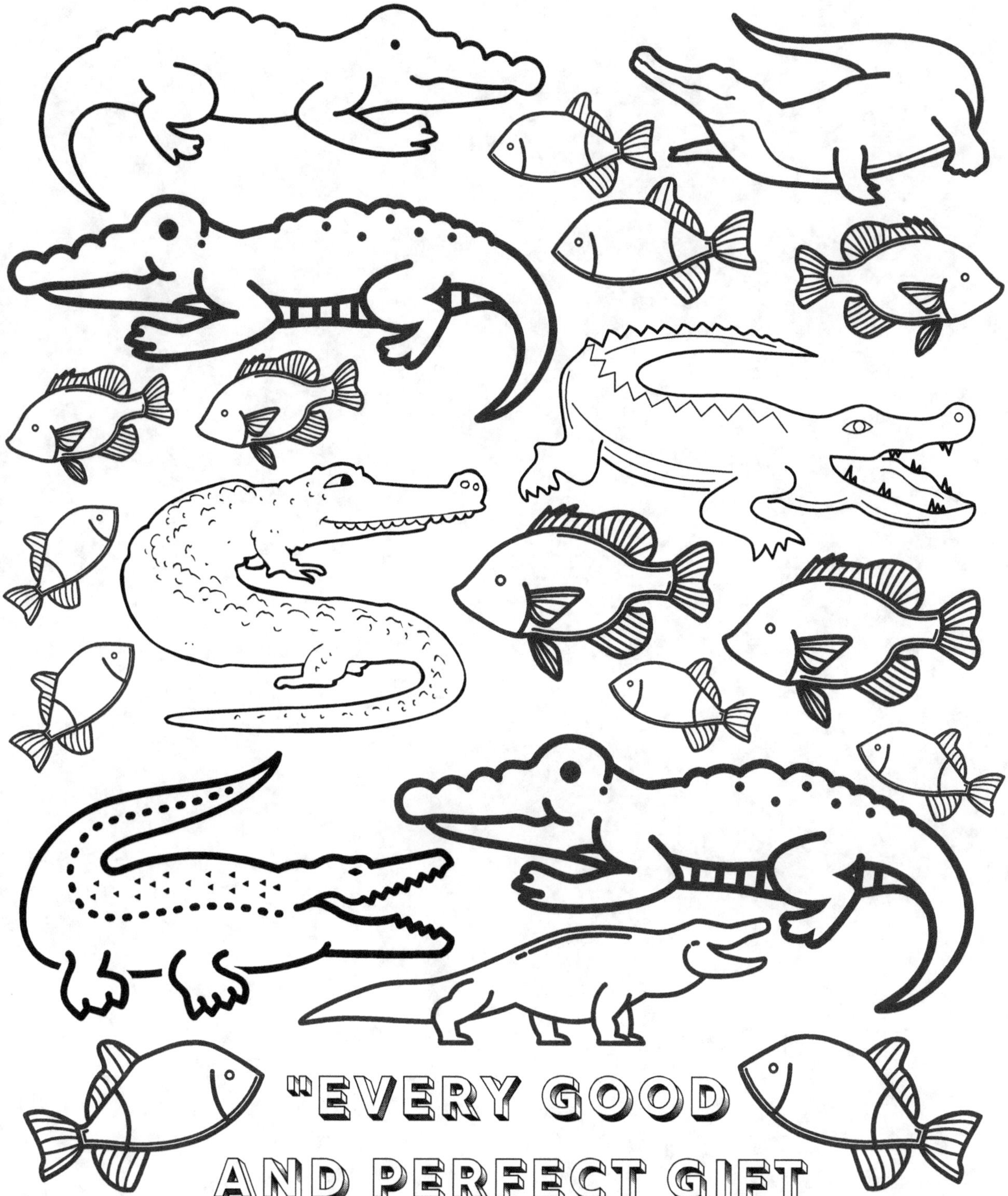

"EVERY GOOD AND PERFECT GIFT IS FROM ABOVE."

JAMES 1:17

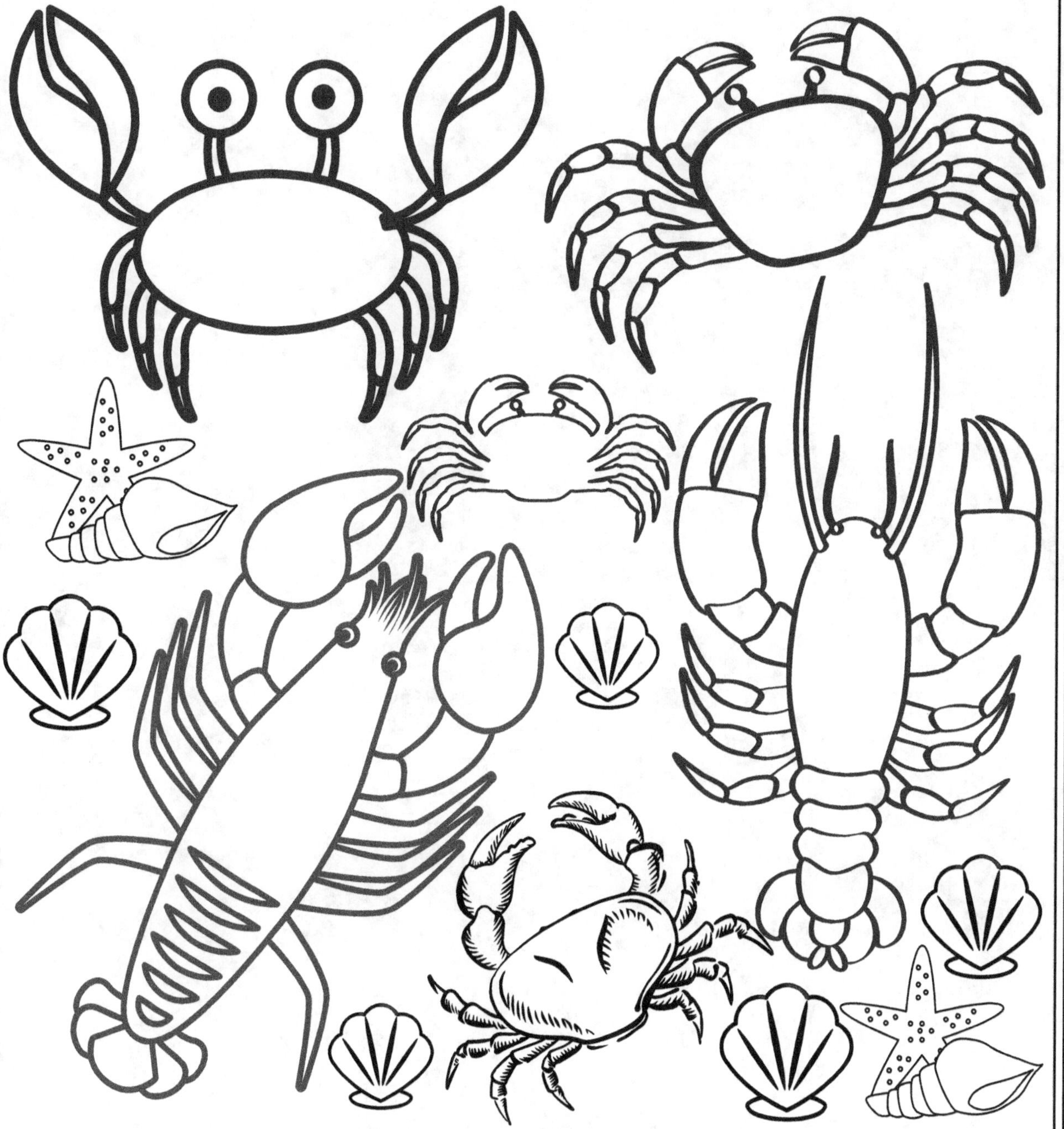

" THIS IS THE DAY THE LORD HAS MADE; LET US REJOICE AND BE GLAD IN IT."

PSALM 118:24

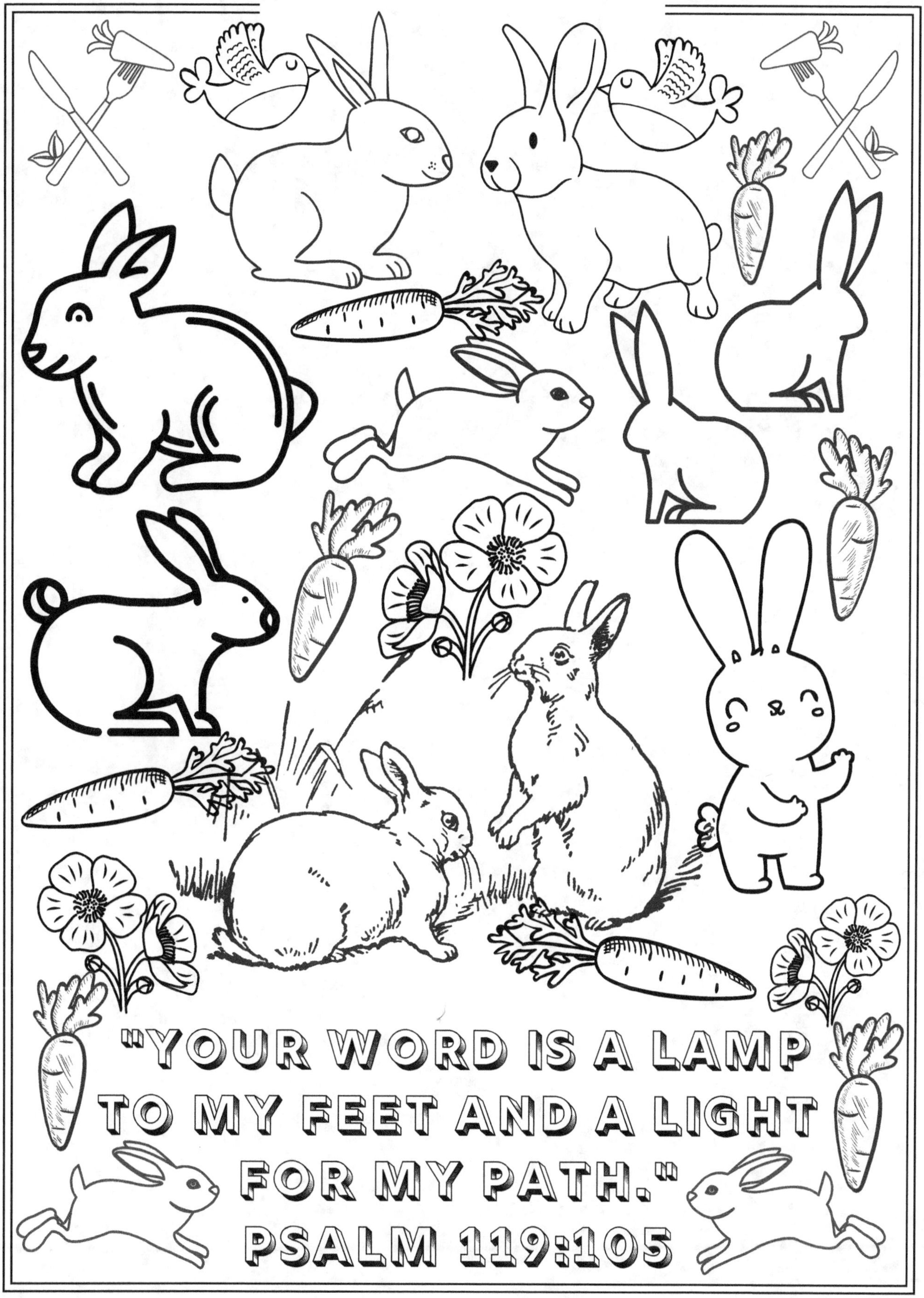
"YOUR WORD IS A LAMP
TO MY FEET AND A LIGHT
FOR MY PATH."
PSALM 119:105

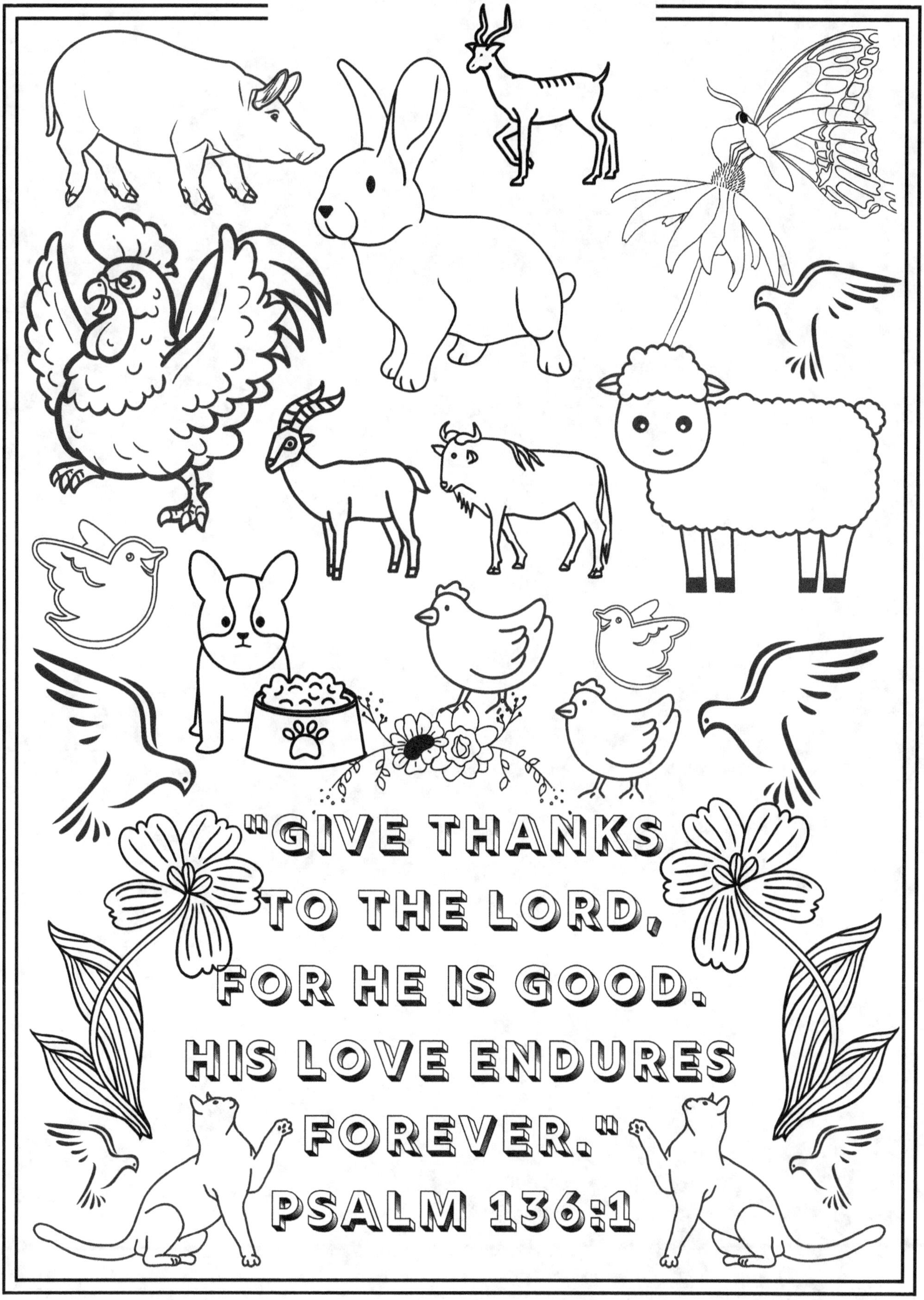
"GIVE THANKS
TO THE LORD,
FOR HE IS GOOD.
HIS LOVE ENDURES
FOREVER."
PSALM 136:1

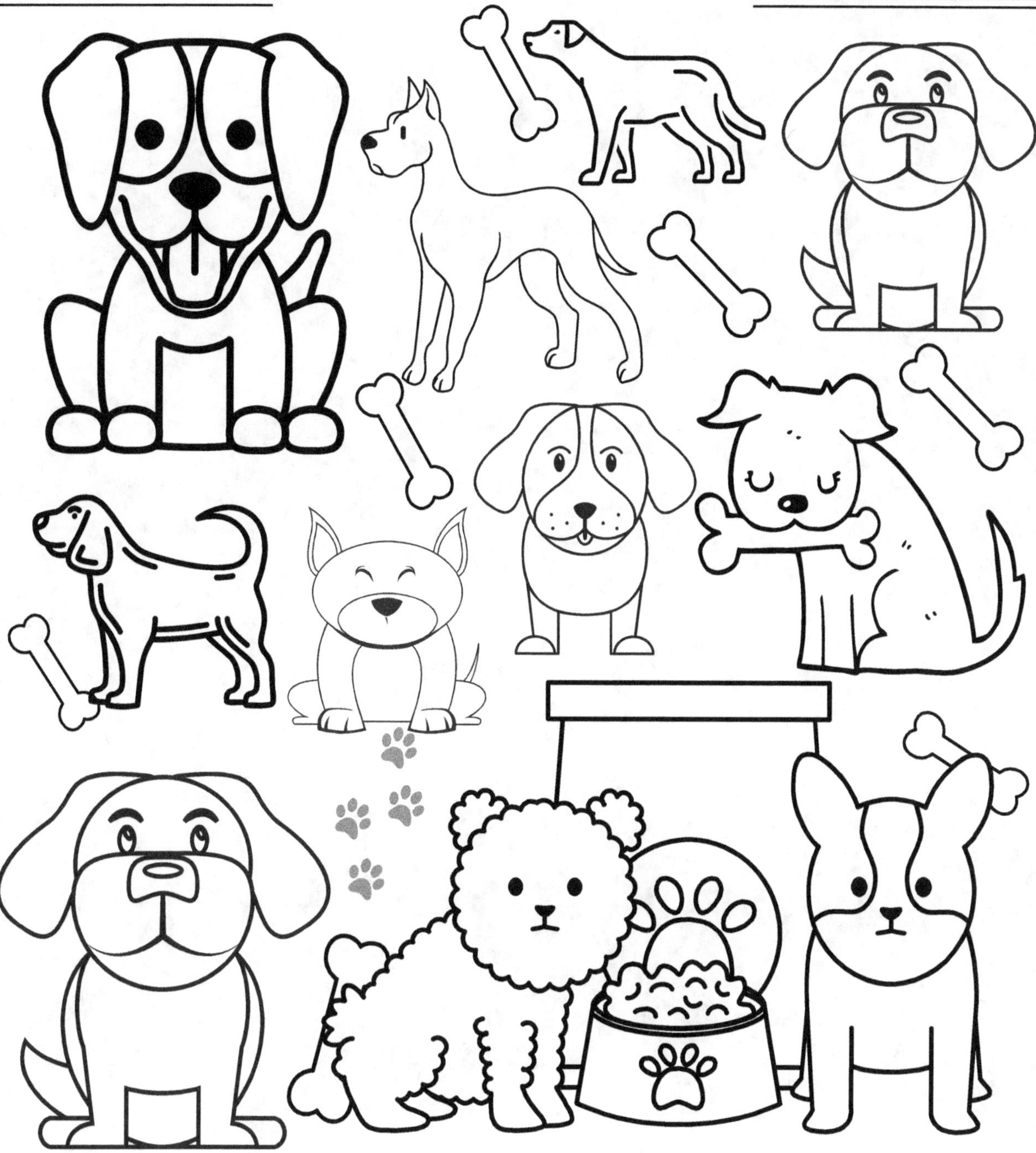

"DO UNTO OTHERS AS YOU WOULD HAVE THEM DO UNTO YOU."

LUKE 6:31

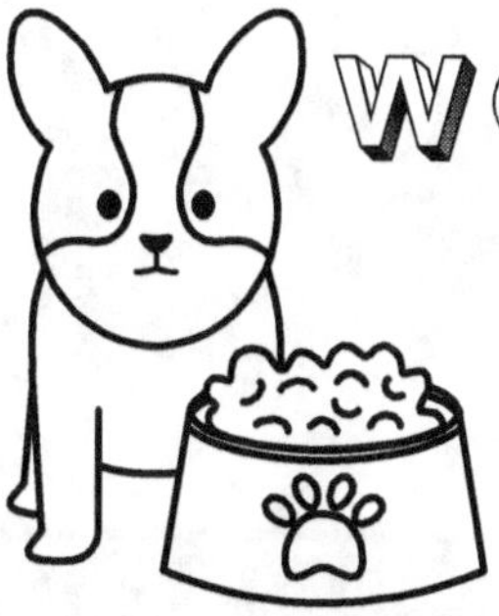

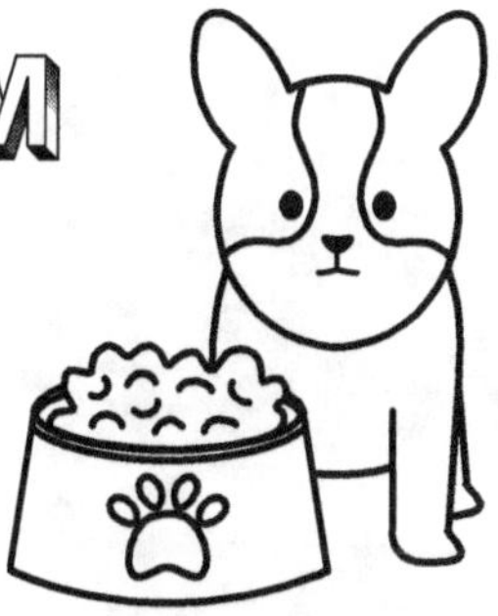

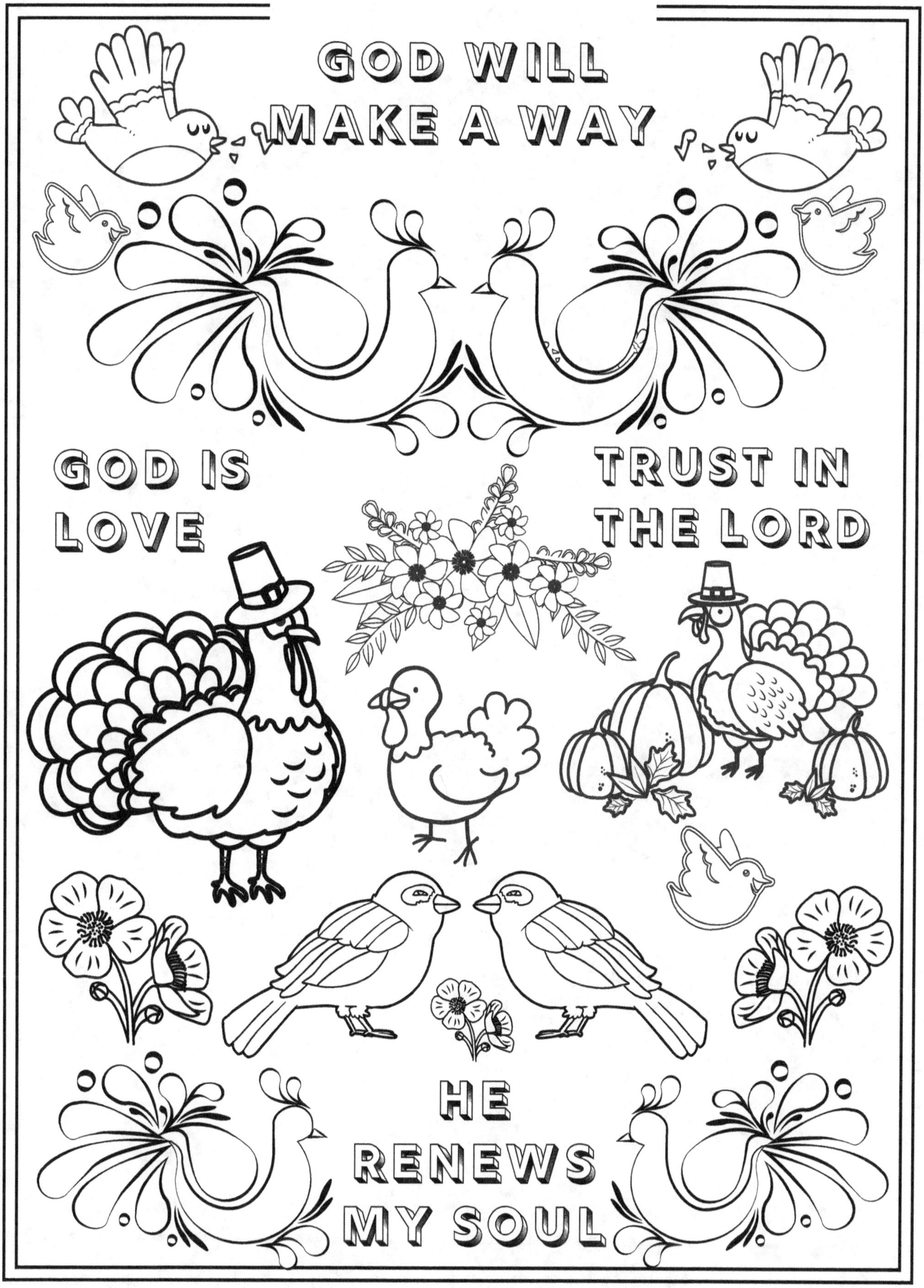
GOD WILL MAKE A WAY
GOD IS LOVE
TRUST IN THE LORD
HE RENEWS MY SOUL

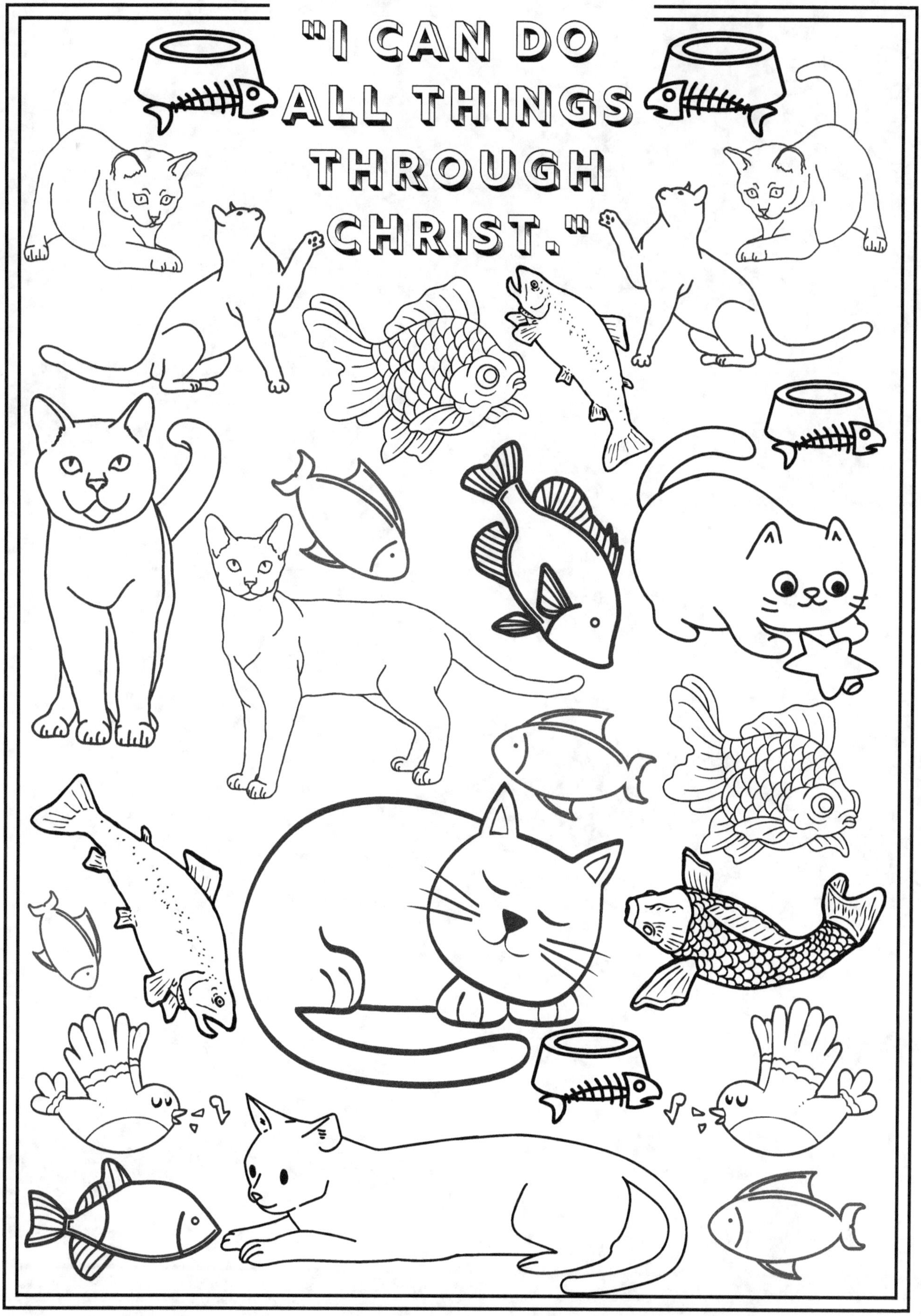
"I CAN DO
ALL THINGS
THROUGH
CHRIST."

"I AM ALWAYS WITH YOU."
MATTHEW 28:20

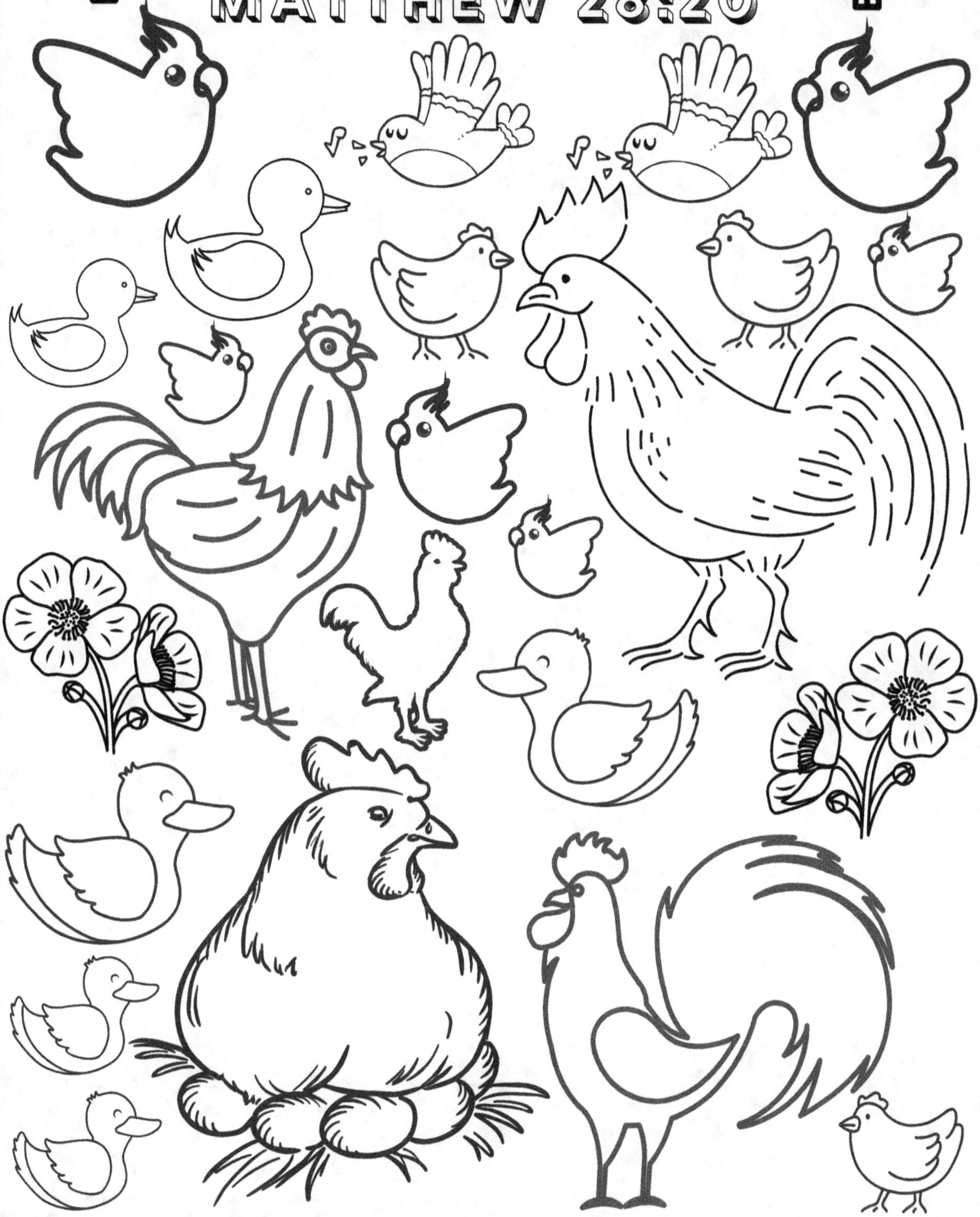

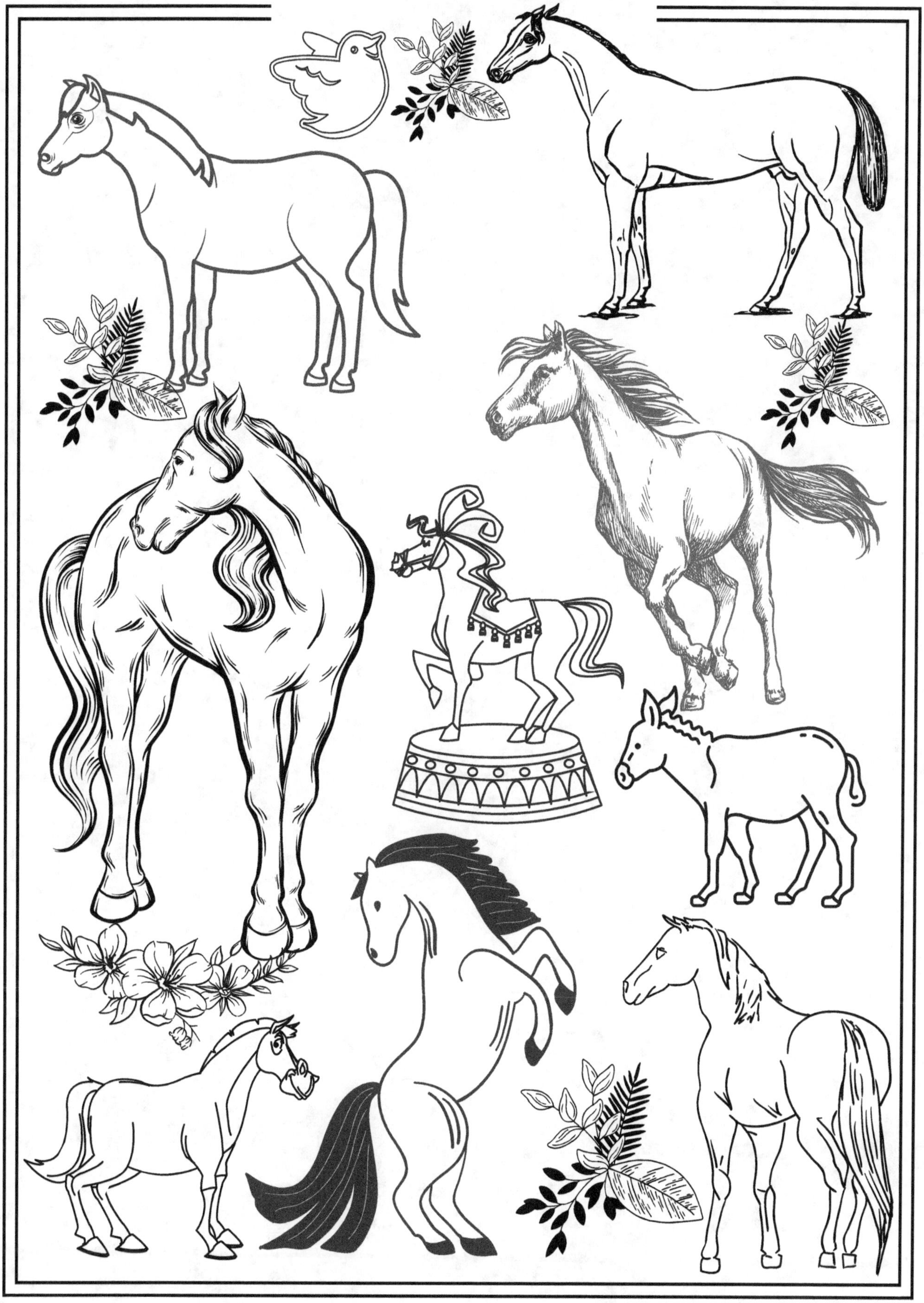

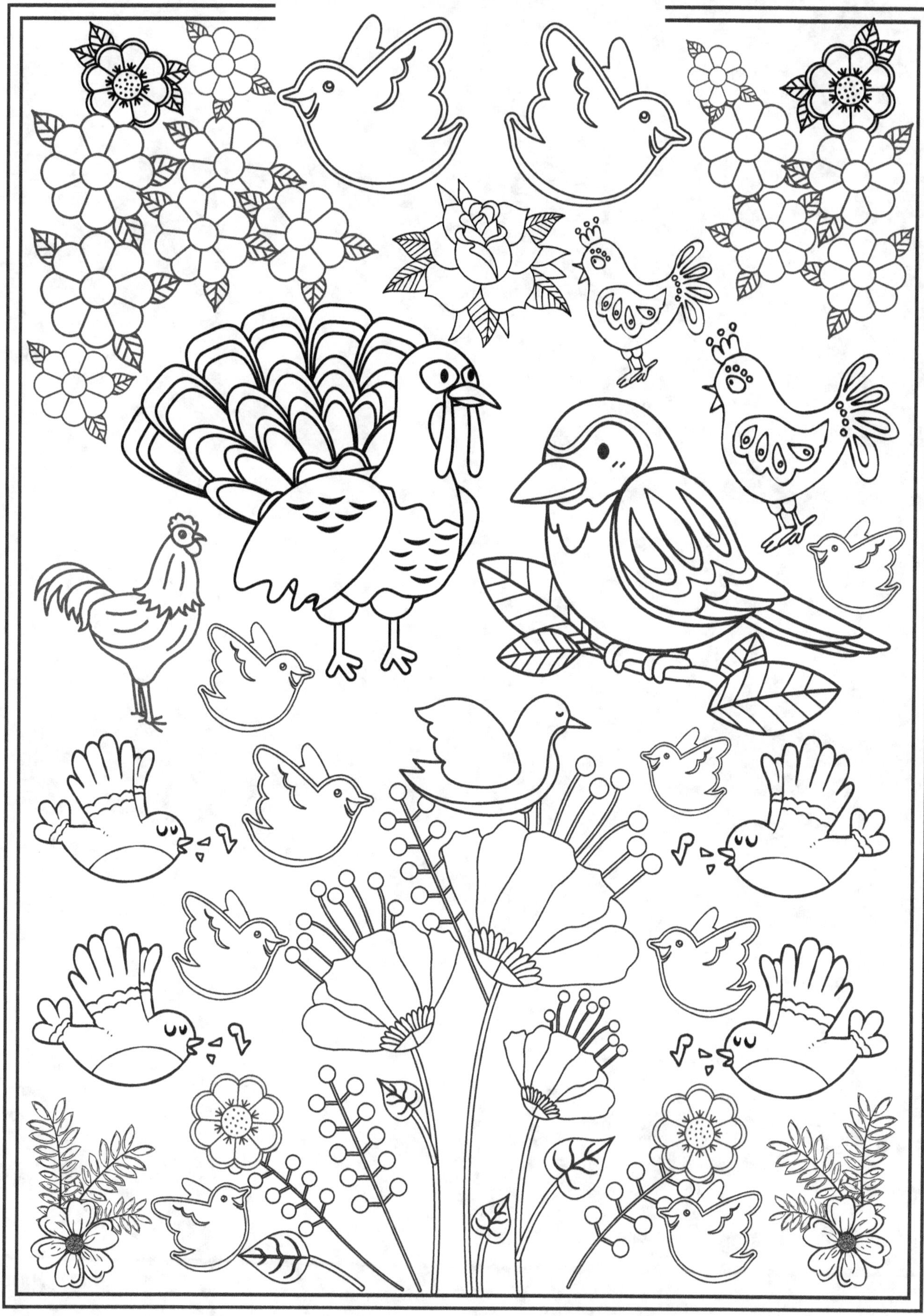

Drawing Paper

Drawing Paper

Drawing Paper

www.ingramcontent.com/pod-product-compliance
Lightning Source LLC
Chambersburg PA
CBHW081456220526
45466CB00008B/2669
* 9 7 8 1 6 5 4 3 7 9 8 1 0 *